What business leaders have to

MW00768310

TRUE WEALTH
... By The Book

Truly Inspiring! *Today more than ever before, we need role models and examples of leaders with values, ethics and morals based upon Biblical principles. I've bought and given away 400 copies and intend to continue to do so.*
- John Perry, CEO, *Medical Development Group*

Every business owner and employee should read this great book. All business success comes from Christian principles, whether the CEO understands them or not. It's simple and powerful – it inspired me even more and confirmed my faith.
- Dwight Cenac, President & CEO,
***Welcome Home Health Care,* and**
Chairman, *Home Health Care Association of America*

This book helped me gain a better perspective on some business decisions I need to make. It is encouraging to read how successful executives discovered God's plan for their businesses and their lives.
- Jerry D. Winkler, President,
Delta Information Systems

This is a wonderful book, so refreshing and different. Too many Christian books are preachy, while this one backs up Godly principles with enlightening and touching stories we can all relate to.
- James R. Young, *President, Young Land Group*

A Very Special Story...

Add your story here...

Join hundreds of people who have given this book as a gift to friends, employees, bosses, customers, suppliers and others.

Add your story or testimony in this space (110 words or less, Bookman font, 11 point). Simply type your story on an Avery 5164 label, (3 1/3 x 4), and place it here with your signature.

For orders of 50 or more, call our office, and we will help you.

Many more encouraging stories inside!

TRUE WEALTH

...By The Book

*How 100 Inspirational
Americans encountered
Character, Moral, and
Spiritual Truths*

by
John F. Beehner

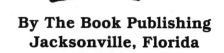

**By The Book Publishing
Jacksonville, Florida**

True Wealth ...By The Book
©Copyright 1999 by John F. Beehner

Formerly Titled:
How To Get Rich... By The Book

By the Book Publishing
One San Jose Place, Suite One
Jacksonville, Florida 32257

ISBN:
0-9655745-2-0
Library of Congress Catalog Number
97-94519
Printed in The United States of America

Layout and cover design:
Lion of Judah Enterprises,
1-800-573-3505
In colaboration with
Desktop Miracles

For bulk quantities phone toll free
888–847–3861

TABLE OF CONTENTS

Acknowledgments

Many people have given me encouragement and support in making this book possible. I am sincerely thankful for their help. It would have been impossible without them. I want to recognize as many of them as possible.

I especially want to thank God for leading me to and through every inch. My prayer is that this book will accomplish His purposes. I also want to say a special thanks to my wife Judy who has supported me and who has been very understanding. I will love her all the days of my life. In addition to the many who contributed personal stories and who are mentioned in the contents, I want to salute the following people as **"Encouragers"**.

Al Bertani, Jim Bleech, Jim Brewer, Bennett Brown, Nita Carr, John Cavanagh, Mark Charboneau, Chuck Coker, Jim England Lee Evans, Sandy Fisher, John Fuller, Lloyd Groves, Bill Hopf, Gary Howe, Pat Kelly, Chip MacGregor, Bill McCombes, David Miller, Dan Murphy, Larry Nichols, Tom Noton, Norb and Marie Novocin, Dr. Victor Oliver, Frank Orlando, Freddie Pierce, John Rumbach, Paul Schwend, Charles "Red" Scott, Ken Soud, Jay Strack, Steve Strang, Jeanie Tebeau, Billie Tucker, Jarda & Sara Tusek, Frost Weaver, and my mom and dad.

The following people have been **"Supporters"** and deserve recognition as well:

Bob & Priscilla Baldwin, Kelli Bass, Deanna Berg, Denny Brown, Susan Carlson, Arthur Carnes, Bud Carter, Larry Cassidy, Peter Chamberlain, Rex Coryell, Joe Day, Howard Dayton, Jerry Deley, Jim Dodd, Steve Douglass, Bob Downing, Larry Elliott, Bob Erdman, Christi Foster, Teresa Foster, Paul Fritsch, Gary Gibbs, Bob Grano, Ben Goldsmith, Tom Grimm, Lloyd Groves, Steve Gyland, Bill Hall, Steve Hall, Dennis Hensley, Susan Hill, Tom Hill, Rick Houcek, Dave Humphrey, Bob Jackson, Ron Jenson, John Johnson, Robin King, Kouri, Jon Krug, Pete Lakey, Paul Landry, John McCollister, Linda McDowell, Col. Nimrod McNair, Frank Maguire, Joe Marino, Erik Mayo, Jim Miller, Ray Miller, Bobby Mitchell, Jack Mitchell, David Moore, Cork Motsett, Randy Overfield, Ken Overman, Buddy Pilgrim, Loren Rozeboom, Mick St. Jean, Larry Schneider, Mike Schneider, David Smith, John Smith, Ted Sprague, Dan Stanley, Gil Stricklin, Peter Sullivan, Pete Tinesz, John Vandiest, Ken Vensel, Denis Waitley, Bert Watson, Bob Watson, Don Wass, Kell Williams, Steven Wolcott, Kaye Woods, Kathy Yanni, Jim Young, Dennis Zink, Librarians from the City of Jacksonville Public Library and the First Baptist Church Library, Jacksonville, Florida.

PREFACE

It was just before dinner at our annual International Conference of peers in a business that I had devoted my life to for 12 years. People from around the world had gathered, and probably 25 of the nearly 150 Executives there would be recognized for different accomplishments. I went to my knees to say a quick prayer before I left for dinner. I was a little tense, thinking I might get a special award and had prepared nothing to say should it be given to me. In the prayer I said, *Lord, am I going to get this award?* Then I heard a small still voice say, *No.*

I spent the early part of my career chasing the American dream as I understood it, wanting to have the riches of money, power and recognition. I was what people called a "moral person" who was enthusiastic, hard working, and visionary. I had moved my family five times in ten years, always looking for greener pastures, moving to bigger successes, but not really recognizing that I was on a false quest for the "world's view" of success. I had a basic belief in God, but could see no relevance of Him in my daily life. I felt if I was just a good person one day we would meet in Heaven.

Yet in starting my second business, I was struggling then, I had an incredible experience or a "divine intervention," and

I surrendered my life to His leading. He led me to a business that works with CEOs of companies with a give-and-take, round-table approach using outside speakers, combined with a one-on-one process. It was the most outstanding and practical business experience anyone could ask for. I learned more through that process than many people will learn in two lifetimes. At the same time, I was effective enough to create a licensed business with a staff of 20 and over 300 clients and associates.

Through the journey, I became personally involved with some of the most successful entrepreneurs and had an opportunity to learn from their experience. This gave me a very broad understanding of how businesses effectively work. I learned to put my faith in Him, but after years of success, I came to realize that I was off course from His leading. I called it God's wake-up call. I had much more to learn about my faith in Him and how to probe the "deeper" things about success and life's purposes.

After dinner that same night in my hotel room while removing my jacket, I can remember it as if it were right at this moment—I said, *Lord, how come I didn't get that award?* Then a small soft voice responded, *Because you are too prideful to think you should receive it and they are too prideful to give it to you.* That answer sunk deep into my heart and I understood. The voice continued, *You need to write a book on this.* And I said, *Lord, a book, no...a chapter, maybe.*

Here I am over a year later, having sold the majority interest in my business and having prayed, labored and researched the book you are now reading. Let me make one thing very clear—I am a messenger and not an author. He is the author and I have just done my best to be humble and open enough to be led to share the contents of the cornerstones truths that not only affect business but also dictate our personal lives. I'm not patient or detailed enough to do this without Him teaching and guiding me. It has been both a big "stretch" and an honor to do this.

John F. Beehner, CEO
The Believers, Inc.

**THE TRUTH
AND ITS
CONSEQUENCES**

The Show of Shows

Not long ago Larry King, the master T.V. interviewer, was recognized on his anniversary show. This time he was the guest and was interviewed by numerous celebrities who were able to ask him their own questions. Question like, who was your favorite guest, most unusual, etc.

The last question posed to Larry by the interviewer was — *If you could ask God a question*, what *would it be?* Larry thought for a quick moment and then said, *Did you really have a Son?* and *Why do so many people suffer?*

So we are going to <u>pretend</u> that Larry King and his producer are going to try to pull off the "show of shows" in the year 2000 in recognition of the birth of Christ by interviewing God Himself. And so it happened, the "miracle of miracles" became a reality. Larry called on his good friend, Billy Graham, who made a direct contact with God and they set up satellite transmission with Heaven.

Larry decided that this time he was going to ask God, *Why aren't more people wealthy?*

Larry opens the show by saying, *Ladies and gentleman, tonight we have the show that you have all been waiting for. It* is my honor and pleasure to welcome to our show, direct from Heaven, God Himself. After some further fanfare and niceties (and a fuzzy picture from Heaven with an outline of Jesus and many of His angels hovering around), Larry gets back into his tough interviewing mode and kicks off with...

"God, why are so many people poor and only a handful of people rich? Wouldn't you like everyone to be rich?"

God says, *Sure! I want everyone to experience riches. I love everyone the same — after all, I uniquely created each person. My love is the purest of love. I created man to love Him and be loved in return. I love Ayatollah Khomeini of Iran as much as I love Billy Graham or the Pope. I love the sinner as much as the saved. However, I cannot love the sin; it is not My way. Yet, I am there at each person's side waiting and wanting to be more active to bless each person.*

Larry comes back with, "Well then why don't you bless everyone in the same way?"

God replies, *Because I have designed the world around My image. I am a Spirit of love, truth, and light, and people who don't live by My truths won't be as blessed as those who do. I am a God of order and truth. My principles are man's highest form of order. They apply to individuals, families, organizations, and nations. Man does the same when he creates his games of sport. He requires that there be order, rules, procedures, and penalties. Businesses, individuals, and families have rules and order as well. Even in a free society like America there must be rules or there would be chaos.*

What is Truth?

God is a Spirit of love, truth, and light.

Truths are the highest form of law, principle or rules.

Jesus brought the spirit of the truth (Holy Spirit) and a deeper insight into the purpose of each principle.

NOTE: "Personal Study Guide" at the back of the book.

I do not change. My truths are the same today as at Creation. Man is in search of Me but often looking in the wrong places, yet I am His fixed point of reference.

Yet, I do not even require that everyone know all My rules to be rewarded, just to live by them and they will experience good fruit in their lives. Many people copy the ways of those they hold in high esteem, but unfortunately no one lives by all My standards of success. All people mix principles of both good and evil.

> **Truth is Truth,**
> **whether you**
> **believe it or not.**
> **Truth is truth,**
> **whether you**
> **like it or not.**
> **Truth is truth,**
> **whether you have**
> **heard it or not.**
> **Frank Peretti**

When you throw a ball in the air it comes down more quickly than when it was thrown up because of the law of gravity. But in My ways if you obey My truths, such as sincerely asking forgiveness of someone you are prejudiced of....four things can happen. You are changed on the inside, the other person's perspective changes, your relationship improves, and I may bless you with a job promotion. I control the timing and type of blessing. Your timetable is not Mine - - I can see the future and big picture.

Larry asks, "What about Your view of time?"

Man thinks short term. I control and focus on the long term and allow negative events as a teaching tool for My purposes. Diamonds are made under pressure and fire can forge steel. Allowing trying experiences makes man stronger and ultimately teaches him that I am in control. Man needs to trust me.

Larry comments, "Aren't you too tough on people?"

God smiles and says, *No, remember, Larry, as the Creator and one and only true God, I am Holy and righteous. I created and designed the whole world system. 'Righteous' means I cannot tell a lie or go back on my word. My long term desire is for all of my sons and daughters to join me in the Kingdom of Heaven. Heaven is not the same as earth. To enter Heaven people need only to be forgiven and cleansed from their mistakes, but many never accept my path. So,*

*My desire is for people like you to tell them why or how to
live a Godly life. There is an eternity where your soul (mind
and personality) and spirit will live with Me forever. Much
of life is about preparing for Heaven.*

**Larry comes back with, "So, this physical life is just on
the job training where we are to stumble around to
figure out your system on our own, right?"**

God says, *No, Larry. It is a matter of faith and belief. My Bible
has the answers, yet a man without a spiritual relationship
with Me cannot accept the answers and explanations that
come from Me. They appear to be foolishness to him. If he
can't see it in a physical sense, he rejects it, but I am an
invisible Spirit on earth and man needs spiritual
discernment to see, sense, and truly understand My ways.*

The Book - The Best Seller Every Year

A typical "Best Seller" book may sell 2 million
copies in a year. But the Bible, according to the
American Bible Society, sold 44 million copies in
1991 in Christian book stores alone.

Estimates are as high as 60-70 million Bibles
sold every year in America, and the numbers are
climbing. One in five Americans buys a new Bible
every year.

Why? The Bible was written by the Holy Spirit
through and to the heart. It is often referred to as
the "owner's manual for life."

It touches the heart with wisdom and
discernment for every man and woman who
sincerely believes and seeks the "Author."

**Larry says, "Why don't you just communicate with us face-
to-face or get on T.V. more often or send us an E-mail
so we can understand?"**

God says, *Larry, as the expression goes, 'I've been there, done*

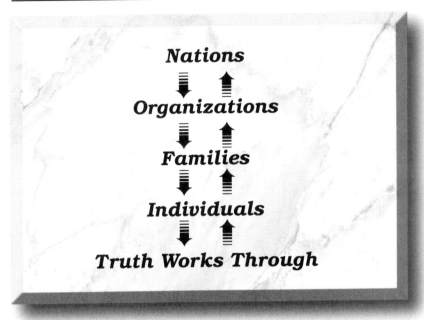

Nations

Organizations

Families

Individuals

Truth Works Through

that!' It doesn't work with man. I spent the first two thousand years working with man as recorded in the Old Testament. I spoke directly to man, sent him prophets, asked man to sacrifice animals to prove his love for Me and still he did not understand or live by the simple principles I gave him. So many men believe the lies, false gods, or enticements of the evil one. His lies appeal to man's ego and pride and self-centered nature.

Larry again says, "So, is this where Jesus comes in?"

God replies, *Yes, Larry, I sent Jesus, My Son, to be a role model, teacher, and to be a sacrifice for mankind. After I had demonstrated to man that he could not really be happy without My presence, and it was time for Me to break the power of evil without breaking My word. This gives man a way to reject evil's grasp. I had men prophecy that Jesus would come in the form of a man to pay the ultimate price so I would forgive mankind once and for all for their mistakes and misunderstanding of not following My purposes. This time, I was not asking man for a sacrifice. I gave the greatest sacrifice possible for any man — My Son's life and His blood. In other words, Jesus brought grace and forgiveness to mankind allowing the Holy Spirit to work in the lives of My people.*

Larry asks, "Why 2000 years ago?"

God responds, *Before Jesus, man was making very little progress. Man struggled to live by My laws. The grace Jesus brought allowed me to place a covering over those who seek My ways and protect them from evil.*

Larry looks at his notes and starts to say, "We are off track from my original question, but before we get back to the subject of riches, tell me more about these truths you keep referring to. I would consider myself a good man, good enough to get into Heaven — so give us some examples.

God says, *Okay, Larry, let me illustrate it this way. If you wanted to build a building or, better yet, even a business that will last for generations, you would have to start with a solid foundation. Right? That foundation must begin with at least three cornerstone blocks. Well, in the life of individuals, families, organizations, and even nations, two of the blocks are about Character and Moral truth.*

*First, I laid out for man the **Character Truths** (C) in the Book of Genesis. Some call them My original commandments. They focus on My expectations for man living on earth to take on My image, nature, and character. Next I expected man to be fruitful through his own initiative; creating and investing according to the different talents that I give him with vigor and good work ethic. Finally I expected man to rule over every living creature. In other words, to be a leader in all aspects of his life.*

Next, as part of the Ten Commandments brought down by Moses I gave man **Moral Truths** ($\mathcal{M}$). Jesus summarized these truths as 'Love your neighbor as yourself' which is synonymous with The Golden Rule (do unto others as you would have them do unto you). More specifically I was expecting man to love and respect his fellowman beginning with his father, mother, and family, to take on forgiveness as exemplified by Jesus, being loyal, with a giving nature, with honesty and appreciation and encouragement for others.

Here is what happens when those two truths connect and engage. Individuals, families, businesses, and even nations exchange talents, work, products, services for the needs and values of their fellowman, creating an exchange of money. The more often and more consistently with the highest quality, it increases the opportunity to make more money and provide more services for both parties. This is what you and your producers have been doing with your show. As you use your talents with entertaining guests, you serve those who watch your show with the potential to buy the products advertised. So the more people you serve, the more prosperous you and your people become in a nation which affords you that opportunity.

"So that's how people get rich," Larry continues. "You are blessing those people who do that well, sincerely using their talents and ability in serving the customer's needs or desires. If Moses and Jesus said these things, how come it took us so long for guys like Peter Drucker and Tom Peters to start coining phrases to talk about "focusing on the customer's needs?" Larry ponders and says, "So why aren't other nations as prosperous or have as many opportunities to be rich as we seem to have?"

God continues, *That is an excellent question, Larry. You are right. America is more prosperous. In fact, you have 6% of the world's population and 54% of its wealth. America is different because of the faithfulness and obedience of the founders that I sent to form your nation. I'm using America as an example for the world. America was founded on Judeo-Christian principles. Just review these statistics with me.*

IN INDIA, PEOPLE ARE SUFFERING WITH ONLY $1360 PER YEAR PER CAPITA. *

IN CHINA, I'M OUTLAWED SO THE AVERAGE PERSON HAS ONLY $2500 PER YEAR, TO SPEND.

IN RUSSIA, AFTER THE WALL FELL FROM THE WEIGHT OF ITS SIN, MORE PEOPLE ARE COMING TO KNOW ME, BUT MY PEOPLE SUFFER WITH ONLY $4820 PER YEAR.

IN JAPAN, AFTER WORLD WAR II, THEIR HUMILITY OPENED THE DOOR FOR LEARNING MY PRINCIPLES FROM AMERICANS, SO THEY ARE MORE PROSPEROUS AT $20,200 PER YEAR.

FINALLY, THE UNITED STATES IS BETTER AT USING MY TRUTHS. THE $25,850 PER YEAR SHOWS THEY'RE LEADING BUT THE OPPORTUNITY TO BECOME MORE PROSPEROUS IS MUCH, MUCH GREATER.

* (World Fact Book 1995/Annual Gross Domestic Product per capita.)

> **Success in life is not about acquiring wealth, but becoming rich from the inside out.**

Larry, unfortunately nations and people suffer by having false gods or not following My principles which lead to more meaningful and even eco-nomically productive lives. As the world gets smaller it is part of My plan to use America's understanding of these truths so more nations will have the opportunity for their people to be prosperous.

But, Larry, let me make one thing very clear. Money is not My primary concern. At times money is a result of doing the right things, but it is an effect, not a cause. Money is not eternal. It is a measure and a tool, but not My standard for success. Money can be a blessing as well as curse. It is temporary only to be used on earth. We don't need it in Heaven. Also, My principles of economic exchange can work for evil as well. You will see liars or thieves make a lot of money as they use their talents and take advantage of their customers. But this is only temporary as the weight of their sins become so great that they will eventually suffer, as they fail to repent.

Larry pauses and says, "Okay, I think I've got that, but You said there were three cornerstones, so what is the third?"

> *God created man incomplete so he needed Him.*

God smiles and replies, *Larry, the third is the most important of all. It is the Chief Cornerstone for any foundation. It is about* **Spiritual Truth** *(S). These are the first four truths of My Ten Commandments. They focus on having an individual and personal relationship with Me by trusting Me as your God, allowing Me to convict your heart and receive forgiveness, using your tongue for goodness, and finally resting and abiding in Me as we grow closer together. Larry, this is the secret to real RICHES. It is about having the full sensitivity, and understanding of true love, peace, joy, and fulfillment in your life - - it's worth more than any gold. Grasping this Truth will change one's perspective about life and My purposes in either a rich man or a poor man.*

Let me give you a notable example. J. C. Penney built his business using his individual and **Character** *Truths of his associates linking them with the* **Moral** *truths of loving his fellow man, the customer. (You will note, his first store was called The Golden Rule Store). He learned these values from his mother and father. I gave him the vision and talent to build a great business on the true desires I placed in his heart. I was there with him day by day, spiritually leading him. He became very wealthy. Yet it was through a down period in his life that he reconciled his need and hunger to draw closer to Me. As you know, his legacy lives on. (reference story in Chapter 15).*

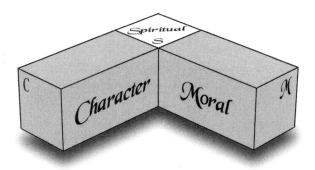

I don't want to be a God of last resort or miracles. I desire for My children to come to Me in a daily loving relationship. Apart from me, man is unfulfilled.

Larry says, "Okay, I think I've got the picture, God, but there is still a lot of pain in the world. I still can't quite understand why that is."

God smiles, *Well, Larry, I can see why people enjoy your show. You get to the heart of the matter. I have blessed you with great talent.*

Your answer is found in the Book of Genesis. It began with Adam and Eve, who are your original father and mother and for all mankind. I loved them both and sincerely enjoyed our time together in the Garden of Eden. I talked with them each day about nature, life's purposes, and the beginning of the human race. I loved them so and shared many of My secrets about My creation, plants, and animals and many other things.

*I warned them about things like poison ivy, marijuana, dangerous animals, and a tree which I called the '**tree of knowledge of good and evil.**' I told them in time I would explain the real meaning of the tree as they matured, but I asked them to promise to never eat the fruit from this tree or they would die of the spirit and sever our relationship. They agreed. I explained about the fallen angel named Lucifer (satan) and his goal to destroy all of my creations. I told them*

> **The Will of God is the Truth of God.**

he was a liar, could not be trusted, and that life outside the Garden was different, but in time I would prepare them for it.

> *Like a fish out of water,*
> *Man was not designed to be apart from God*

As they grew older they started to take on what many would describe as a **'teenager attitude.'** They became more opinionated and didn't appreciate My teaching. They believed I could be wrong. They wanted to find out things for themselves and be on their own.

One day in the Garden when Eve was gathering food, she came upon the 'tree of knowledge of good and evil.' Wrapped around the tree and impersonating a snake was the evil one, satan. Using his most appealing voice he started a conversation with her. He subtly persuaded her to listen to him and said, 'Why don't you try some fruit from this tree?' She said, 'I can't, God has forbidden us to eat from that tree. He said we would die from its fruit.' Satan replied, 'Aren't you and Adam fed up with God telling you what to do all the time? There is a big beautiful world out there and I have seen it all. Aren't you fed up with being trapped here? The 'grass is much greener' in other places. I will help you and show you great forests, rivers, mountains, and gold like you have never seen before. You can be your own king. You know God loves you and will protect you. Surely He won't let you die. He has wonderful plans for you and your children. Why not try a little bite of this fruit? It won't hurt you and you will love the taste. It is sweeter than anything you have ever had — plus there is a lot more outside of this little garden.'

So Eve took a bite and shared it with Adam, telling him about the things that satan told her. Disgusted Adam said, 'It is just as well, I am so fed up with God anyway. We know he won't let us die. He loves us too much. If He kicks us out of here, maybe we will get to see some of those great things satan was talking about.'

Larry says, "So what did you think?"

When they told me what they had done, I was very upset. I finally said, 'okay, you want to go it alone and follow the promises and lies of satan. You need to learn on your own, so I will give you your own free will — the will to choose between My will and your own. You can be your own God, your own parent, your own king. Because I cannot lie or break My own covenant, you must leave the Garden of Eden.

> *Above all, love deeply by His Truths because love covers a multitude of sins*

Adam, you will face hard labor in the fields, and Eve, you will face great pain through the labor of having children. You will have to learn through emptiness, pain, suffering, and adversity in a world apart from Me. I will always love you and be near you. I must now remove My abiding spirit from you because I cannot coexist in an unclean heart. Spiritually you and your children will be dead. I am holy and cannot abide in a person who is self-centered or has other gods before Me. You will have to sincerely want and ask Me to come back and spiritually abide in your heart. You will not see Me but many times I will often protect you. I will not interfere with your choice of free will. You will need your fellowman because I will make men and women with different talents, capabilities, and desires. You will never know true love, peace, joy, or your full purpose without Me.

Your choice will mean that apart from my truths, the world will be self-centered and focus on evil.

In My way and in My timing I will give man truths to live by and send the Messiah, My Son, to break satan's stronghold for the eventual saving of the world.

Quietly Larry asks, "So God, there is pain in the world because of man's choice to follow evil, is that right?"

Yes, man chose his path. I did not choose it for him, but in time I will rectify it. For now, man has a choice to individually and collectively follow My ways and be God-centered or follow his ways and be self-centered. Yes, there are many so-called "good" people in the world who follow many of My truths who think they have the answers to life, yet miss out on a much "Richer" life through me. Unfortunately many of them are not looking to Me for help to solve their pain, frustration, anxiety, or adversity; they choose the "quick fixes" (such as aspirin, drugs, or drinking, recreation or even more work) suggested by society. Even when they get a "wake-up" call they focus on symptoms rather than the root cause which is spiritual, not physical or mental.

You cannot break the laws of God, you can only break yourself against them.

Larry concludes, "As expected, God, this is very enlightening. Unfortunately our 90 minute show must come to a close. I know your comments have changed my perspective and those of many of our viewers. Thank you for creating the world and giving us an opportunity to be here and to serve You. As we promised, this was the show of shows. We hope to hear more from you, God."

God says, *Larry, the time is growing short for the return of My Son. I urge you and your friends to seek Me through the lives and witnesses of your fellow men who call themselves Believers.*

Knowledge and the application of Truth is a more important form of currency than money.

After the show concluded that night, in his dressing room, Larry pondered the things he had heard and felt an urging in his heart to pick up this book and begin with Chapter I.

THE MORAL:

There is an absolute correlation between the patterns of our lives and the principles the Bible urges us to live by.

Character
Truths

In the book of Genesis in the Bible, God revealed the creation of heaven and earth and His creation of man and woman in His own image. He gave us dominion over earth expecting us to be fruitful, to take the initiative of creating, and investing for growth, using our God given talents by the sweat of our labor. Finally, He told us to rule over every living creature, leading by example over the physical and mental aspects of life.

Ultimately He still rules over the spiritual world, which we must learn to interact with to achieve His purposes and receive a peaceful and fulfilling life.

These Character Truths coupled with the proper application of the Moral Truths, are the foundation keys to prosperity and business success.

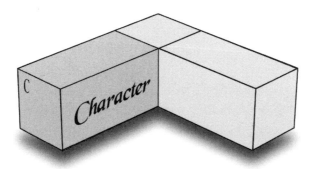

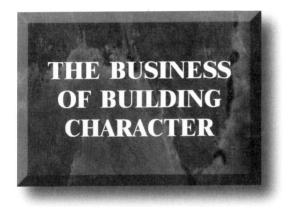

THE BUSINESS OF BUILDING CHARACTER

Character Truth: *God Created Man In His Image.*

Character Quality: *Take on His Character of Love, Truth and Light.*

Seven Years of Preparation

Henry P. Crowell was raised in Cleveland, Ohio in the 1860s. His father was a shoe merchant who tragically died of tuberculosis at only 43 years of age. The family was devastated, and Henry's dream to attend Yale University was dashed, as he had inherited the potential for the same disease. Just a few years later, because of fears for his life, his family doctor insisted he must "go west" and live outdoors for seven years.

Henry had recently made a commitment to serve God in whatever he did. Friends had prayed with him to seek God's will for his life. He realized the Biblical significance of the doctor's "seven-year" order, and believed there was a divine purpose for his struggles to breathe normally.

The next seven years were frustrating, living away from his family. Henry worked odd jobs on ranches and farms and traveled. He gained experience in business by buying, planting and selling two farms in North Dakota. Henry pledged that, if the Lord would allow him to make money, he would keep his own name off the business, so God would get the glory.

As he finally returned home, Henry prayed that the Lord would provide him with a business of his own. Within thirty days, he was offered the opportunity to buy an old, run-down mill near Akron, Ohio. Adversity had taught him to draw close to God, to listen for His voice and be open for His leading. He felt God leading him to buy this old mill. Little did he know that the mill would become a giant, and a legend in the food industry, known today as the Quaker Oats Company.

Could Cancer Be A Blessing?

Few sports fans will ever forget the performance of Dave Dravecky of the San Francisco Giants baseball team a few years ago. Because of cancer, part of his left pitching arm had to be removed. He made a well-publicized comeback, only to break his arm in the second game. The cancer had returned and the family agreed with the doctor that the best decision was to amputate his arm.

Today Dave says, *Cancer has been a blessing. God has given me an opportunity to share His love with so many different people because of my circumstances. You know, a valley for a farmer is a very rich place to plant a crop. When we go through the valleys of life, it is very rich for each of us. Unfortunately, my pride got in my way. I just wanted to be in control. But through my suffering I have become more like Him. He shapes us and molds us in the way He wants us to be. Suffering produces perseverance—perseverance*

> *I thank God for my handicaps, for through them, I have found myself, my work and my God.*
>
> **Helen Keller**

CHARACTER QUALITY

- Take on His Character of Love, Truth and Light -

The word character originates from a Greek word that means to "chisel." You mold your character by how you respond to circumstances and people. God wants us to take on His character of love.

In 1728, Benjamin Franklin was on a personal quest. With all his study and research, he concluded that happiness should be our ultimate goal in life and that it could only be attained through correct actions. He picked 13 virtues that he would do his best to live by each day. He developed a score card he used each day. He exemplified the men of character that shaped our national future, who believed in honesty, humility, justice and the Golden Rule. Today, many live by the philosophy of "me-ism," my rights, self interest, quick fixes, and short-cuts to personal success without sincere regard for others.

Our creator is calling us to take on His image, nature and character of Love (toward Him and one another), Truth (His principles), and Light (His path for our lives). As we do these things, we honor Him.

The number one purpose of a business is not to make a profit, but to take on and exemplify His character to others. Unless we know Him intimately and follow His ways, we are destined to learn through circumstances and trials. If we heed these experiences, we will eventually learn His ways and our character will come closer to His image.

produces character—and character produces hope. Hope will not disappoint us, through and with Him. We are all in-process. He is the healer. Through this experience I have learned to look at life from an eternal perspective.

Working the Principle

J. C. Penney's father was a farmer and a pastor, while his mother was a devoted homemaker in a small town in Missouri. During his early retail experience, Jim was offered a partnership in a new store in Kemmerer, Wyoming, known as The Golden Rule Store. Little did he know that the principle, *Do unto others as you would have them to do unto you,* which he learned from his father and early partners would set the tone for a retail business still flourishing today.

He would later say it was the teaching of his parents that he followed: *When a man works with a principle, that principle makes him representative of a great working force. He need never be anxious. The creative power of the universe is behind him. He is working not for anyone, but a principle is working for him. His success is assured.*

As Jim began to employ people and lay down his principles, he came to the conclusion that *making money must always be a by-product of building the character of men and women and the rendering of essential service to mankind.*

HOW CLOSE?

In an interview, Billy Graham was asked by a reporter, *Since you are so blessed by God, why do you think He would allow you to get Parkinson's disease?* Billy replied, *I guess He wants me to draw closer to Him.*

Changing Lives

Truett Cathy is considered a "non-conformist" in business circles because of his convictions and character. In 1946, he founded Chick-Fil-A, now a $400 million company that does its very best to live by its principles and beliefs. Truett openly shares what he thinks are the three key ways we can "change the lives" of those we lead, manage or just interact with:

1. By our instruction—what we say.

2. By our influence—what we do.

3. By our image—what we are and what we stand for.

In other words, changing lives takes precedence over making money. Profit is merely a by-product of producing good people.

Chick-Fil-A is one of the few retail businesses located in malls throughout the country that is closed on Sundays because Truett still believes in observing the Sabbath and encouraging employees to grow spiritually. Truett has been teaching Sunday School to 13-year-olds for 40 years. Not long ago an attorney from Atlanta, who was in his class as a teen told him, *I remember very little about what you said in Sunday School but I do remember that you brought me some chocolate pudding to my house when I was sick.* Truett continued, *He remembered what I did. Kids, like adults, will copy us. We all teach character and values at work as well as at home.*

He reminded his listeners, *We are created in the image of God and it is up to us to do our very best in all our circumstances. I tell young people, this is a do-it-yourself world. You can't blame your parents for your circumstances. We all start from an uneven playing field; life doesn't always seem fair.*

The Real Dream

> *Ability will help a man to go to the top, but it takes character to keep him there.*

History will never forget the passionate speech of Martin Luther King when he said, *I have a dream that my four little children will one day live in a nation where they will not be judged by the color of their skin but by the content of their character.* For each of us it becomes a question of finding our higher purpose. Then we must allow God to build our character, strengthen our spirit, and inspire our love to pursue it.

Martin Luther King learned his character from the spiritual convictions of his father and mother and his pastoral training at seminary. As we study his traits, we see that he exemplified the character and image of Christ. Jesus took the approach of loving, teaching and modeling truth. He was willing to sacrifice himself for the greater calling of God.

Had Martin not taken the Christian, non-violent approach, he would have never found his place in history and made such great progress for his people. His approach serves as another example for all of mankind that love will always win over hate.

If You Knew The Future

If God gave you His plan for your future, how would you react? Jim Brewer, business counselor, says, *Most of us would say, but God, I can't do that. I'm not qualified. So He leads us one step at a time until our character and confidence develops — until we finally discover and realize this is what we are supposed to do. The wise person then stops to reflect and thank God for the journey, and for not telling him what he would not believe.*

Role Models

Charles Barkley, the great NBA star, said on TV commercials, *I am not your kid's role model.* But like it or not, kids with or without a father have for years idolized athletes. It used to be that the media did not hunger to report the negative or criminal activities of heroes. Today, it is front page news as a result of the erosion of values and positive character traits and as a result of the pursuit of negative news.

Reggie White, the outstanding NFL football player and ordained preacher, is a man who has used both his influence and money to "walk his talk." He has been an inspiration to thousands, an individual we can all look up to. Reggie said, *Playing football is helping me in my spiritual life. It is helping me build character. People cry out for role models. The problem is that in our society a lot of our kids are choosing the wrong heroes. We should be looking for the ones who have character, the ones who seek Him and humble themselves to a higher calling and a superior being. They are the ones who are going to have a stronger character than probably anybody you will meet.*

The Corporate Coach

Jim Miller is CEO of a $100 million office supply firm that has 57% market share in the Dallas/Fort Worth area. He authored a highly respected and practical book called *The Corporate Coach*. When you get face-to-face with Jim and ask him what motivates him to still be in his business he says, *It is the fact that I just love to see people grow and develop their character and aptitudes. That's what thrills me. I have seen hourly people grow from young and inexperienced to vice-presidents and partners in the company. I refuse to be called CEO because my real job is being the coach. If you love, care, grow and counsel people, help them stretch themselves and develop their character, the sales and profits will follow.*

> **Character:**
>
> *Our strength is shown in the things we stand for; Our weakness is shown in the things we fall for.*

Hiring Smart

Red Scott is an icon in business, one of those unique individuals and personalities who took a $30 million business to $2 billion in 15 years. Yet he took time to humbly share his cardinal principles with thousands of business executives throughout the country.

> *Who you are is more important than what you know.*
>
> **Ed Ryan**

His expertise was in mergers and acquisitions, growing companies for future sale. Hiring Presidents of companies became critical as he and his team bought businesses. He said, *We were looking for superstars in 'game-breaker' positions, (just like a key position on an athletic team, such as a great quarterback or linebacker, that could make or break the ability of a team to win). At that level, we were doing our best to* **hire smart** *by putting candidates through intensive interviewing and screening processes. One of the most over-*

riding qualities we looked for in individuals was the level and maturity of their character. I am gun-shy to hire people who have not been through significant learning experiences in their lives and bounced back–what some people would call 'the school of hard knocks.' Candidates without the right character qualities were the first to be screened out.

Red Scott, along with the late Sam Walton, are among the few high profile CEOs who have openly acknowledged their belief in God and their belief that faith in God and regular worship is critical to an executive's character.

The Risk Takers

In 1959, Ada, Michigan, became the birthplace of a company that today does over $5 billion annually, offering over 10,000 quality products and services through nearly a million worldwide distributors. Rich DeVos and Jay Van Andel pioneered the multi-level industry marketing concept , and are estimated to have helped more people start their own small business than anyone else in the world.

Amway's first credo states that: *We believe that every man, woman and child is created in God's image and because of that each has a worth, dignity and unique potential. Therefore, we can dream great dreams for ourselves and others!*

While 80% of American small businesses fail in 5 years, these risk-taking small business owners create the majority of jobs every year. Nothing builds character faster in an individual than starting his own business. We all have talents but not all the talents we need to be successful alone. Small business offers the opportunity for individual initiative and fuels risk-taking, innovation, competition, competitive pricing, and niche marketing. It stretches people to come to grips with their desires, will, and determination—all spiritual traits which God uses to further our character growth for a higher purpose.

The Winningest Coach

Only one man has been inducted in the College Basketball Hall of Fame as both player and coach. After coaching for 40 years and winning 82% of his games, he said that *winning isn't everything.* He used all of his abilities and resources to help mold young men into individuals of character. He taught the principles of fair play, integrity, respect for others, discipline (teaching his players to leave basketball on the court), and living a balanced life.

> *He is more interested in making us what we ought to be than in giving us what we think we ought to have.*

John Wooden shared this creed with his players and fellow coaches:

1. **Be true to yourself , your talents and convictions.**
2. **Make each day your masterpiece by doing your best.**
3. **Help others because it is better to give than to receive.**
4. **Make friendship a fine art.**
5. **Build a shelter for a rainy day trusting God and your fellow man.**
6. **Drink deeply from The Good Book and other writings each day.**
7. **Every day pray for guidance and give thanks.**

How could one coach from UCLA be so consistent and win more championships than anyone else in basketball history? Because his simple values came from the right source of knowledge and truth. Was he wise or blessed, or both?

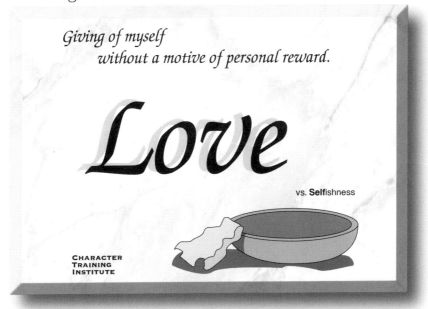

Giving of myself without a motive of personal reward.

Love

vs. **Sel**fishness

CHARACTER
TRAINING
INSTITUTE

11

Hard Lessons

Joe Gibbs, the Hall of Fame and former football coach of the Washington Redskins, shares publicly how God has worked through his life. During the earlier tenure of his time in Washington, he decided that he needed to be an "aggressive businessman" during the off season to be able to make money for his future security and personal wealth. He said, *I got into an Oklahoma land deal. It personally 'wiped me out.' It was against my wife's better judgment and without prayer that I made the decision. Unfortunately it was my pride and ego. I learned more about myself during that time. God built my character and He loved me through it all and miraculously I avoided bankruptcy and publicity.* The lesson Joe learned was that he had not known or focused on God's plan for his life. Sometimes these lessons are expensive and take us to the brink.

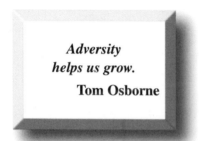

Adversity helps us grow.

Tom Osborne

A New Start

Shortly after the fall of the Iron Curtain, the Russian Ministry of Education asked Campus Crusade For Christ and a number of other American ministries to help their teachers and students acquire the principles that seem to make America great. They told the Russians that they would have to allow the Bible in the classroom after more than seventy years of official state atheism. Without much hesitation, the Russians complied and a new ministry called "Co-Mission" was created. Over three thousand Russian teachers have been trained by 350 American volunteers who spend anywhere from three weeks to a year training teachers and assisting in the classrooms. Their mission is called

A man wrapped up in himself makes a very small package.

"Character Training," taking the principles from the Bible to teach and share about honesty, integrity, commitment, initiative, and self-discipline. The program has received so much good publicity and success that many Americans are asking their public school districts to do the same.

Humbleness Builds Character

Through the annals of history, God always seems to use the humble to accomplish eternal tasks. Why does He only use the humble (open, teachable, listeners) and obedient?

Because they are not saddled by excessive concern for material wealth, self-aggrandizing or the worldly entrapments which block their spirit from hearing His voice.

Here are a few examples of the humble who have changed the world:

Noah	Joseph
12 Disciples	Abraham
Moses	Martin Luther King, Jr.
Billy Graham	Mother Teresa
Henry Ford	Joan of Arc
George Washington	Ben Franklin
Ronald Reagan	Abraham Lincoln
Knute Rockne	Alexander Graham Bell
Albert Einstein	Gandhi
Dag Hammarskjöld	Helen Keller
Pope John Paul	Norman Vincent Peale
James Madison	Albert Schweitzer
Winston Churchill	Bill Bright
James Dobson	Robert Schuller
Franklin Roosevelt	Dwight Eisenhower
Walt Disney	

Turn Around

In the 1970's, Bob Rosof, a successful contractor, had retired to his boat in Tampa Bay, Florida. He was asked by a judge (and personal friend) to take a teenager on board to determine what he could do to help turn him around rather than send him to jail. Today, Bob is again retired from Associated Marine Institute, the organization he created, which continues to work in 42 national locations to help turn around the lives of approximately 2500 young adults who have been sentenced by courts. The story of Associated Marine Institute is a well-documented one. It has been reported by national television, featured in *Parade* magazine and has received national media coverage when American presidents came to visit. Because of the efforts of AMI, 80% of the kids who go through the programs stay out of jail. The program builds the character they never learned at home.

Character First

Over the last twenty years the oil industry has had a number of booms and busts which have made it very difficult for Tom Hill to keep his people motivated to the highest level of productivity and quality. Tom Hill runs Kimray, a $25 million, third generation manufacturing firm with 250 employees in Oklahoma City. They manufacture regulators and control valves for the oil industry. More than the ups and downs of the business, Tom noticed the attitudes and work ethics of those he hired never seemed to be as good as years earlier.

He is holy and does not conform to a standard, He is the standard.

He began to work with Bill Gothard of the Institute for Basic Life Principles in Oak Brook, Illinois, and they developed a program called Character First. They identified 49 Biblical character traits (some might call them attitudes) that apply to everyday life such as: wisdom, flexibility, punctuality, thoroughness, initiative, dependability, compassion and loyalty. Their belief is that people will repeat behavior that is praised, as taught in Ken Blanchard's *One Minute Manager* approach of "catching people doing things right." Over the last four years employees have been recognized in monthly company meetings, not for their individual performance, but for exhibiting special character contributions to the company's success. Supervisors present the awards and describe the character exhibited by the individual. As their concept developed they started using the same traits in their hiring practices.

The concept seems to be working because personnel problems are down 80%, profit margins are up, sales are up, and profits are at record levels even though the cost of raw materials and labor have increased significantly. They had an 80% reduction in worker's compensation costs, and employee bonuses last year were 12.5% of their annual salaries. Kimray has dropped its quality control program and become a leader in its industry by having the highest warranties and fewest returns.

But even more satisfying to Tom Hill is the morale difference that he notices in his people.

> *The closer we come to Him, the more we become like Him.*

He believes that *my purpose is to honor my Creator and use my business to serve my employees and their families in building their character, strengthening them as individuals, and nurturing their household.* No, he hasn't forgotten the customer or making a profit... they are just not #1 on his list of priorities (They are #1A).

He has also begun a movement to teach other companies how to adopt these principles in their own businesses. Tom says, *Character and attitude start from within a person's heart, so they are more fundamental than attempting to manipulate behavior from the top down. Many people today are not taught the same character traits in the home as they were in the 1950's. It is part of our purpose and what God has laid on my heart to do. We've got to do our part to rebuild America's fiber.*

Paradoxes of a Person of God

Strong enough to be weak;
Successful enough to fail;
Wise enough to say, "I don't know;"
Right enough to say, "I'm wrong;"
Compassionate enough to discipline;
Mature enough to be childlike;
Planned enough to be spontaneous;
Great enough to be anonymous;
Stable enough to cry;
Leading enough to serve.

Barry Morrow

THE MORAL OF THE STORIES

1. We are to learn from our circumstances, handicaps, and adversity to take on His image, nature, and character in preparation for an eternal life.

2. We are not created to be alone. He loves us and wants to be loved in return through our journey. That is the simple purpose of life.

3. We all teach character, values, and attitudes by what we say and do, both at home and at work, where the majority of adults spend the greatest share of their waking hours.

4. Character is defined in the Bible through Scripture, stories, examples, and parables. God's image is love, truth, and light.

5. For many of us, we have a hard time breaking out of our "comfortable lifestyle." He is asking each of us to depend on Him, to take on the risk of living out His character traits each day. We are constantly in character development, all our lives. If we listen, He speaks through these circumstances.

6. People with the right character are more teachable and reach toward the depths of life.

Answers To Prayer

According to business counselor, Jim Brewer, prayer is answered by God in three ways:

A. *Yes, I've been waiting for you to ask. This will be a good experience for you in preparation for My greater plan in your life.*

B. *No, this is not right for you.*

C. *Wait, your character and heart need to grow and mature.*

God looks at the motives of our prayers and actions, whether they are right or wrong for us. All of these answers build character and our faith.

7. Most employers say that their greatest asset is their people. However, they focus on profits to reach their goals and to impress themselves and their stockholders. Profits come and go, but the character of people is eternal. Without the good character of our employees there is no customer or profits. God's timeframe is long, and His blessings follow our actions toward His purpose and His people.

8. His image is long term. He is calling us to set aside the quick fixes, instant success shortcuts, and desires of the world, and look to His ways which may take longer because we grow in character from the experience.

9. In my twenty years of owning businesses and counseling and learning from successful CEOs, consultants, and their experiences, I've concluded that a positive company culture and "walking the talk" by executives and workers alike are the most important internal factors in business productivity, profitability, and the character of a company.

Character Defined

Leaders of companies teach character values by "walking their talk." Below are the 49 character traits "biblically based" that the Character Training Institute recommends for recognizing employees for demonstrating and contributing to a company's success:

Alertness	*Faith*	*Patience*
Attentiveness	*Flexibility*	*Persuasiveness*
Availability	*Forgiveness*	*Punctuality*
Boldness	*Generosity*	*Resourcefulness*
Cautiousness	*Gentleness*	*Responsibility*
Compassion	*Gratefulness*	*Reverence*
Contentment	*Hospitality*	*Security*
Creativity	*Humility*	*Self-Control*
Decisiveness	*Initiative*	*Sensitivity*
Deference	*Joyfulness*	*Sincerity*
Dependability	*Justice*	*Thoroughness*
Determination	*Love*	*Thriftiness*
Diligence	*Loyalty*	*Tolerance*
Discernment	*Meekness*	*Truthfulness*
Discretion	*Obedience*	*Virtue*
Endurance	*Orderliness*	*Wisdom*
Enthusiasm		

10. Families are the first character school/training for our children.

11. The character of our children is the leading indication of our nation's future.

A WORLD OF CHANGE

Character Truth: *Be fruitful and increase.*

Character Quality: *Create and Invest for Growth.*

The Change in Communication

- In 1800, delivery of a letter sent coast-to-coast in America could easily take months by stagecoach to reach its destination.

- In 1860, it took several weeks by Pony Express.

- In 1869, it took a week or so by train.

- In 1920, delivery of that same letter took only a few days by plane.

- In 1960 it was overnight by jet.

- Since the mid 1980s, it takes just a few seconds by FAX.

- Today we have instant communication through E-Mail plus same-day delivery of hard copy information.

> *Plans are often worthless,*
> *yet the planning process is priceless.*
>
> **Dwight Eisenhower**

Technology is advancing so rapidly that information is globally accessible at lightning speed. The time required for one company to mirror or copy another company's products is exponentially faster than ever before. As a result, product life cycles are being shortened to radically brief periods of time. Changes are occurring at warp speed. It's predicted that the FAX will be obsolete in the next 2 years because of widespread use of the Internet.

The Cycles of Change

In 1900, 95% of Americans lived off the land. By 1950, it was 15%. In the 1920's there were over 100 automobile manufacturers in the United States. By 1950, there were six. We've gone from Mom and Pop corner grocery stores to supermarkets to warehouse super stores.

In the mid 1970's, the leading manufacturer of portable calculators was Bowmar, and the average calculator sold for $125. By the mid 1980's, they were out of business and a

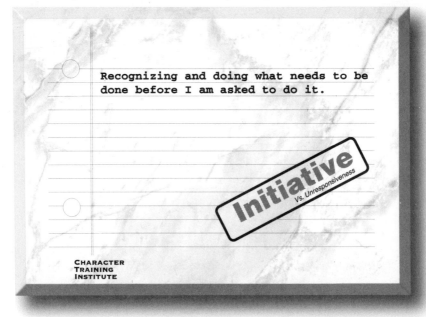

Recognizing and doing what needs to be done before I am asked to do it.

Initiative Vs. Unresponsiveness

CHARACTER TRAINING INSTITUTE

calculator the size of a credit card sold for 80 cents. In the early 1980's, yogurt, computer and video stores were popping up in thousands of small strip retail centers around the country. Within 10-12 years, there were a handful of national companies controlling the market share in these industries.

Products and services are always moving in a cycle of innovation, start-up, rapid growth or failure, maturity, commodity and decline. These are the same cycles of life. All products eventually become commodities, so innovation is absolutely critical to stay even or get ahead.

CHARACTER QUALITY

- *Create and Invest for Growth* -

Human life begins with a seed, and passes through stages of personal or business growth with time tables for fruitfulness and harvest:

- to be prosperous for a year, grow wheat
- to be prosperous for ten years, grow trees
- to be prosperous for a lifetime, grow people
- to be prosperous for an eternity, grow close to God.

By His design, we are charged with taking the initiative, being self-starters and filling this earth with humankind. We are to use our creativity to make life better by ultimately bringing the world's brothers and sisters together as one with Him.

The cycles of change are unstoppable and time is irreplaceable. In the year 1900 experts said knowledge would double every 100 years. Today world wide experts agree that knowledge is doubling every two years. Yet, our Creator gave us Truths so we may gain wisdom, knowledge and discernment.

We have natural, physical and spiritual laws. Sowing, growing and reaping is both natural and spiritual. Our abundance of fruitfulness in the world is by His design. Our world of rapid change is preparing us for something greater.

Resisting Change

The late Bill Oncken, great trainer on the principles of *Managing Management Time* says that *Most people go through life backing into the future, keeping their eyes on the past...the things they have been educated to do and done well, rather than turn around and face the future and openly deal with the unknowns –accepting them as a challenge. There is a resistance in all of us to venture into some new territories. Yet, there is a spiritual guidance system that Our Creator put into each of us, with the intent we would seek Him for confirmation– knowing our talents and capabilities and His purposes which He has placed within us.*

Commitment to be Fruitful

In the early part of this century, an author by the name of Horatio Alger wrote novels that inspired young Americans to overcome life's adversities and hardships—to meet the changing world head-on, with determination, hard work and integrity. His novels inspired thousands to God's calling to reach for successful accomplishments and to help their fellow man. These books were often referred to as the "rags to riches" stories of America.

Without risk (faith), there is no growth.

Dr. Norman Vincent Peale and educator Kenneth Beebe carried on this legacy. Fifty years ago, they formed the Horatio Alger Association to recognize distinguished Americans who have exemplified heroism through their accomplishments. Horatio Alger recipients were men and women like—

- ***James Earl Jones'*** mother and father left him as a young child to be raised by his sharecropping grandparents in Mississippi. When his grandparents moved him to Michigan in search of better schools, the impact on him was dramatic. James began to stutter.

Embarrassed, he seldom spoke in school. One day, for a class assignment, James wrote a poem and turned it in. It was so good that the teacher thought he had plagiarized it. She insisted that, if he had really written it, he must stand before the class and read it verbatim. His honor was at stake. Deep in his spirit, he formed the determination to do it—and he did.

That incident was a turning point in his life. Today, after several hit movies, dramatic stage performances and Emmy awards, James is one of the most sought-after voices for commercials in the United States and is recognized internationally as a legend in his own time.

- **Jim Moran's** father emigrated to the United States from Ireland. He died when Jim was just 14 years old. Jim worked after school to pay his parochial school tuition, and then worked evenings at a gas station. His mother taught him to be on time, keep his word, not to take anything that didn't belong to him, and always do his best.

  Eventually Jim bought the gas station where he worked for $360 and turned it into Chicago's largest Sinclair station. After World War II he returned home. He bought a friend's car for $75; he repaired it and sold it for $275.

  This was the beginning of one of the world's greatest success stories in the automobile industry. Jim was the first to advertise his new auto dealerships on television. Known as *Jim Moran, the Courtesy Man*, he built the largest Ford dealership in the world. Then Jim developed cancer. After surgery, his doctors gave him only a 5% chance to live; but, through the grace of God and Jim's determination, he recovered in his Florida home and started a Toyota distributorship which covers five southeastern states.

- **Ted Turner's** father told him *If you have it tough when you are young, it prepares you better for the rest of life.* His father was tough on Ted, twice sending him away to school as a young boy. He required Ted to read two books a week and made Ted pay room and board at home while working summer jobs. His father wanted him to be a strong, honest, well-educated and competitive man.

After Ted graduated from high school, his mother and father divorced, and his sister died after a long illness. He began working at his father's successful billboard advertising agency; six years later, his father committed suicide. Ted lost his idol and teacher.

After the funeral, Ted learned that his father had sold his business. The new owners offered Ted the opportunity to buy it back for $200,000, which he did not have. Ted struck his first business deal by making the owners his partners instead.

In building his father's business, he discovered his God-given abilities and forged through his tough "life preparation", to do things others said could not be done. He bought a bankrupt television station; in eighteen months, the station began turning a profit, showing reruns of movies and syndicated programs. He bought the Atlanta Braves and Hawks sport franchises and covered their games. Then Ted pioneered in the new cable television industry with his "super station".

The launching of CNN, with a 24-hour news format, was met with predictions of disaster by all the experts. Ted, however, had a vision of a world-wide television and communication system, which became an international coup. CNN has created a smaller world, preparing the world to be the united family which God intended.

Because of his family training and response to hardships, Ted is considered as brash, gutsy and even arrogant. However, by not listening to doubters, Ted became just the kind of man God needed for the communication breakthrough which has set the stage for more to come.

The World Impact

What are the incredible events and circumstances that are causing changes to compound so rapidly? There are three driving forces:

1. Technology derived from the reaping of the harvest from

the American Space Program and other initiatives.

2. Changes in political events focusing on the fall of communism and its impact on our defense spending.

3. Economics and increasing competition as the world is brought closer together.

As we observe these events from a Biblical perspectives, a greater plan appears to be unfolding.

Technology Explosion

By the year 2000 we will double the current number of satellite transmitters that instantaneously send pictures and data throughout the world. Cellular telephone communication will grow faster than any other medium, as underdeveloped countries will use cellular technology rather than spending the time and money to establish underground or overhead wiring and cable systems, replacing phone systems that are archaic and less reliable. Digital TV, digital sound and transmission will improve and increase communications dramatically.

Experience is always the hardest teacher, because you take the test before you learn your lesson.

More and more of us will run our own business from home and use our own satellite dish offering 500 channels from around the world!

Computer access is now world wide with data storage expanding because of increasingly smaller chips with greater capacity, allowing PC computers to maintain entire libraries for internal and external use. Networking for intra-office or intra-company purposes will be maximized within the next few years, tripling communication capacities. The Internet will not only provide communication for E-Mail, but also provide home libraries as well as new access to markets, buying and selling products world-wide. We are just on the threshold of using these techniques.

Political Enlightenment

In 1988 Dr. Scott Thompson spoke to numerous CEO and entrepreneurial groups while he served as a White House advisor. He boldly predicted that within a short time communism would fall. Why? Because of the technology revolution—satellite and computer communications insure that the "truth" would no longer be able to be withheld from the people in communist countries. He predicted an eventual overthrow of those governments. Few CEOs recognized the truth in his predictions, especially after almost 40 years of communist rule in these countries.

> *If you always do what you've always done, you will always get what you've always got.*

Today, nearly 50% of the world's population has turned from communism or dictatorship toward "a free market economy." Only China maintains its communist government, while moving rapidly toward free enterprise with the fastest economic growth of any nation in the world today. As the leaders of these economies continue to learn and understand free market concepts, they will copy American products and services at much lower costs, creating more competition world wide. By the year 2000, for Americans the idea of a smaller world and larger marketplace will be a reality.

Under communism the average individual in the Czech Republic earned under $1,000 per capita per year (communism was a form of state-subsidized welfare). In 1997, just seven years since its new government took charge, the average income is $7,500 per capita.

Reduction of American armed forces has changed America's employment picture. The need to assimilate returning servicemen spurs the creation of more jobs.

Economic Consequences

Where will these new international businessmen go to learn about the free market economy? The United States is the most open society and the most prolific "giver" of information and

> *When God measures a man, He puts the tape around the heart instead of his head.*

knowledge in the world. For years underdeveloped countries have sent their best and brightest to our prestigious schools, but this educational quest will become more of a grass roots business-to-business learning experience in the years to come.

- The information age has produced a boom in business literature (books, magazines, tapes) for large and small businesses over the last thirty years.

- Trade agreements such as NAFTA will grow as we protect our markets and start partnering more with foreign companies in strategic alliances, not only to share knowledge, but also for economic growth opportunities.

- The American service sector took over from the manufacturing sector as the largest employer just a few years ago. We recognize that manufacturing jobs create more economic wealth and require more support employment. Just as the textile industry left Europe and England in the 1800s to move to the New England area of the United States, it moved again to the Carolinas in the 1900s. While many firms still maintain manufacturing in the United States, much production is done overseas in Southeast Asia or has been captured by foreign companies in those marketplaces importing into the USA. The opportunity remains for small and mid size businesses in America to learn and expand their exporting efforts like big businesses have been doing for years. This is the great opportunity for us to be involved in a world marketplace. Yet many smaller entrepreneurs are too "spoiled" by many years of richness in an expanding American marketplace to take new risk in a world market.

- American business will continue to be caught up in the "margin games" to gain the edge and ability to compete

> *The pilgrims gave us the legacy of faith to risk a better life. Today the faith to risk continues to lead people to start a business.*

worldwide when economics are so divergently different from our own. This puts economic pressures even on the company that doesn't do business internationally. Downsizing and re-engineering will remain alternatives to American business leaders. Unfortunately some top executives are using downsizing and economic pressures as an excuse to "look good" to stockholders rather than doing what is right.

What is America's Role?

Interestingly enough, America has been the greatest example of change and obeying the command to be fruitful and increase. Much of this is exemplified through innovations to market and sell products in an economical way. Most of the world uses the English word "marketing" which was invented in the United States, as part of their own vocabulary. Former communist countries are just learning what marketing really means, since

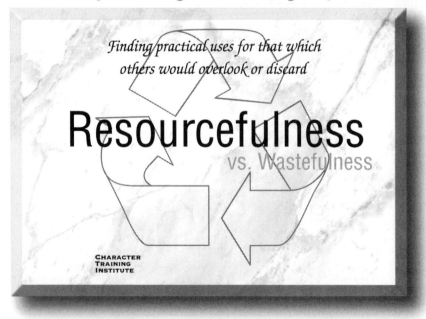

Finding practical uses for that which others would overlook or discard

Resourcefulness
vs. Wastefulness

CHARACTER
TRAINING
INSTITUTE

they formerly were part of state planned economies. The American role will not only be to continue to teach the world the economic principles of a free market economy but to also teach the ethics by which its success is driven. *Customer focus* as a business principle is rooted in the Ten Commandments. When we share ethics, principles and methods, we will be sharing God's truths, teaching others who will be blessed.

> *Not only can you not step in the same place in a river twice, you can never step in the same river twice.*
>
> **Heraclitus**

Bringing Us Together

As technology and the speed of communication, education, and sharing bring us together as a world, the political and economic barriers of doing business together are reduced. In order to do business internationally, the American model, based on morals, must be used for long-term success. This moves the world closer to God's higher standard and opens the door for more spiritual growth.

THE MORAL OF THE STORIES

1. God did not say be dependent upon man or governments. He said to take initiative and risks in order to be fruitful and fill the earth.

2. God is love, truth, and light. With the fall of the Iron Curtain, as these countries work toward building their economic capacity to do business throughout the world, a major barrier has fallen. A communist nation such as China which has been pirating products (e.g.., American videos, software, and CD's) will not be able to continue these practices and have economic viability with the rest of the world. Those

> *Sorrow looks back*
>
> *Worry looks around.*
>
> *Faith looks up.*

who lived under communism and a society of fear are now having to adjust their paradigms and mental thinking to understand the moral truths (i.e., faith is the opposite of fear; honesty is truth) that God set in motion to make the fair exchange of goods and services viable to everyone.

3. Businesses which continue to seek short term profitability may be sacrificing their full potential or gambling with God's eternal purpose for their business. The game of juggling the economics and accounting of a business often results in acquisitions to increase sales volume, cutting costs to improve profitability. Yet the long term future is most important. Tom Phillips, retired CEO of Raytheon, says that *The eternal view would help prevent fantasies of unlimited risk taking for corporations. The eternal view also keeps at bay personal feelings of total devastation when risks appear to be failing.*

4. As we become a media driven society, the deceit we absorb hinders the convictions of many people and impedes God's grace working through us. Our motives will catch up with us. God is looking at the long term and the truth of the heart. His goal is for us to be unselfish and not self-centered.

5. The myth that *the only constant is change* will divert our focus on reality. The truth is God is the only constant. He is the same yesterday, today and tomorrow. His truth is law. As we know Him, we change to become more like Him.

6. What really caused the dramatic fall of the Iron Curtain? There was barely a shot fired, nor was there any significant loss of life. It was like the fall of a house of cards. It seemed to start with simple prayer in churches in Romania that had been closed for years. The political pressures created by the Reagan administration certainly forced Russia to focus upon the economic realities. Did communism fall because of God's hand, the weight of its own sin, American pressure, or all of the above? In the end, righteousness will always win over evil.

7. Is the technology explosion because of man or God? God is facilitating this change to bring us closer together to prepare for His son's return. It is time for each of us to seek life's "owner's manual" (the Bible) and make our own determinations.

> *We are like rubber bands – we have to be stretched to be useful.*
>
> **Dwayne Sumner**

8. The Book of Revelation talks about a time similar to the one that we are experiencing. Those falling away from belief are being more critical and hypocritical, while those coming closer to God are surrendering to Him. Our society is caught up in an interpretation of values and we are picking sides. Weekly church attendance in the U.S.A. is up to 45%, vs. 39% in 1950.

9. A number of people study Bible prophecy. Grant Jeffrey, a businessman from Toronto, Canada, says through his studies and research that there are 38 major Biblical prophecies which must be fulfilled before the return of Christ. As of 1996, all had been fulfilled or were in the process of fulfillment. Is He preparing a way for Jesus to return?

WHAT CAUSES OUR FRUSTRATION?

1. *Not enough of something such as money, status, or love?*

2. *Results from a bad decision we made?*

3. *No long-term perspective for our future?*

4. *Our violation of His Truths and their consequences?*

A HIGHER STANDARD

Character Truth: *Fill and subdue the earth.*

Character Quality: *Put your talents to work.*

Being the Best

Bill McCartney, former head coach for the University of Colorado, won a national championship and has been credited for a new winning standard for their program. Now as Chairman of Promise Keepers, a national Christian men's movement, he often has an opportunity to address men in stadiums around the country and share some of his experiences as well as his walk with the Lord. He publicly shares how he used a method to "bring out the best" in his players once every few years. It was such an intense experience that it is not something that could be repeated often. But he says *When we had to play a nationally ranked team where I just had to pull out all the stops, I would use this technique.*

He would tell all the players in a team meeting on Monday that he was going to be in his office on Wednesday and wanted to meet individually with each player for three minutes only. He said, *Men, I want to know how you are going to perform on game day and what I can expect from you.*

He said it would cause quite a stir among the players as during the next couple of days they stopped to think about how they were going to do their best on game day. When they came into his office he had moved all the furniture away from the center of the room and put two chairs face-to-face only five feet apart. He looked into each player's eyes with intensity and leaned forward to ask, *What kind of performance can I count on you for game day?* He said that the players were so "hyped" by the time that they got to sit nose-to-nose with him, they would discuss how they were going to play their very best, make improvements, or how they would never let him down.

McCartney's response to them was, *John, I am going to hold you to it. I am putting you on your 'honor' to deliver.* Many of these players would not even have an opportunity to play because there were more than 60 players on the team, but they were ready on game day. The intensity permeated the team. McCartney concludes that if you put a good man of character *on his honor* he will deliver.

> *Success is not about winning basketball games but about being faithful.*
>
> **John Wooden**

Eagle Scout

At the age of 13, Sam Walton became an Eagle Scout, at the time the youngest boy in the history of the state of Missouri. Boy Scouts has been an organization through the years built on the whole concept of *On my honor, I will...* His mother motivated Sam by telling him to be the best that he could be in anything he undertook. His family struggled during the Great Depression, but he worked his way through college before going to work for the J. C. Penney Company before he had to enter military service. There he was impressed with the values established through the *Penney idea.* Even though he became the wealthiest man in the world in the

CHARACTER QUALITY

- Put Your Talents to Work -

The door to opportunity is always labeled "push." Our Creator has given us uniqueness and an abundance of resources. He gave us talents, skills, intelligence, personality and physical strengths, and He wants us to aggressively use them. Like any investor, He wants to see our talents maximized by hard work using His principles for true wealth.

Willie Gary and "Rudy" Ruettiger both have something in common. Willie went to college without a dime, hoping to earn a football scholarship. He came from a family of sharecroppers. Willie's father taught him to "work for free" if that is what it takes to get ahead, and he did. He impressed the football coach so much with his attitude that, as a scholarship became available he was given one. Through Willie's hard work he became a lawyer and now is a judge in Florida.

Rudy's story was made into a popular movie. No matter how he was "put down" as too small and an underachiever, he lived out his dream with "heart." God blessed Rudy, and his *never quit* attitude led him to Notre Dame to participate on the football practice squad. The movie portrays his work ethic and unwillingness to quit. He received his degree and now is a highly successful motivational speaker around the country.

Both men worked hard, built their character, and discovered their talents. Their faith brought them through trials. God is calling us to work our mind, exercise our talents, and plant the same principles. They are seeds in the lives of other people.

1980s, through the growth and development of Wal-Mart, Sam never focused on money, material wealth, or possessions. He was driven by the values of focusing on the customer, honesty, hard work, and doing his best for his fellow man.

FIRE AND PRESSURE

Fire destroys forests. Farmers use fire to burn away old crops or mature sugar cane before harvest, yet fabricators use it to make glass or steel. Pressure in the earth over hundreds or thousands of years will form oil, ores, minerals and diamonds.

God uses the same principles sometimes in our lives to mold us and build our character. You may think you are in the middle of a tragedy, but His purpose is to burn away the old for a new crop to be planted in your life. At the same time the pressure may be so great you want to give up before your character and personality have matured to take on a whole new responsibility that you have never dreamed of.

Hold on tight and turn to God and in His time He will reveal the answers and the meaning to our agony. We have to take the first step. We can't see the future and we need to learn patience. It all becomes character building, part of his first laws— take on His image.

Don't accept anything but the best

During the Tonkin Bay situation, Henry Kissinger asked an assistant to prepare an analysis. The assistant worked night and day for a week, and put the document on Mr. Kissinger's desk, only to receive it back within an hour. Affixed to the report was a note asking that it be redone. The assistant dutifully redid it; he slept a total of nine hours for an entire week. The document went back on Mr. Kissinger's desk, and an hour later it was returned with a note assuring that he expected better and asking that the work be done again.

> *Knowledge, apart from faith, is worthless*
>
> **Malcolm Muggeridge**

So the assistant went back to the drawing board once more. Another week of intense work, and then the assistant asked if he might present it personally to Mr. Kissinger. When he came face-to-face with Mr. Kissinger, he said, *Mr. Kissinger, I've spent another sleepless week. This is the best I can do*.

Said Mr. Kissinger, *In that case, now I'll read it.* Sometimes, it seems that God works the same way.

The Talent For Popcorn

Orville Redenbacher was raised on a farm in Indiana, where eating popcorn was a family tradition. As he grew up he had a burning passion to find a better quality popcorn with fewer wasted kernels. Through the years he would peddle his new popcorn on roadside stands and finally attempted to bring it into chain stores. When he reached a point of utter frustration through lack of success, he stopped to think about the things that his mother had told him.

In *Guideposts*, he shared, *Talent, I thought about that for a long time — and what I had done with my abilities since I was a young man. Mom had talked about talents. When I practiced my coronet at home as a youngster she would wince at my bleeping."* She said, *God gave you your share of talents, son, but playing the coronet is not one of them.* He continued, *Yes, God had given me talents. I believed they were from Him. I even taught about talents as a Sunday School teacher. Sometimes the teaching tickled my memory about seeking advisors. I picked up my Bible and rifled through the pages. Yes, there it was...Proverbs 24:6, 'For wise guidance you can wage your war, and in abundance of counselors there is victory.' (RSV).*

Orville drew inspiration from the words and pulled together a team of friends as advisors who encouraged him to seek an advertising agency who came up with the theme, concept and packaging to create the "Orville Redenbacher Gourmet Popcorn" image. It was the turning point in creating a business which set a new standard for the food industry.

Wise Counsel

It is too bad Orville Redenbacher never knew Bob Nourse. Bob helped to operate and finally close down his brother's business of many years. He then struggled for months about what he would do with his life. He saw his experiences as limited to the manufacturing business, but somehow he was fascinated with education and training and had a natural talent for facilitating and listening. He also had a compassion to help others grow and avoid the mistakes that he and many other executives had experienced.

During his struggles to find a new career at 52, he turned to God and went to church every day early in the morning saying, *Oh, God, what am I going to do with my life?* He told his wife that he dreamed *he had a stainless steel tube through which God would send me messages.* With the advice and encouragement of friends he went out one day in the country by himself to seek God's vision and develop a new plan for a business to help CEOs of companies.

That business today has hardly changed from the principles of Bob's vision. The business now operates worldwide and helps CEOs of noncompeting businesses in small groups which gather together one day a month to learn, grow, exchange and sharpen their talents. The business is internationally known as The Executive Committee (TEC) and has over 5,000 members (CEOs and entrepreneurs) internationally. It has been the standard bearer for a whole new service industry, helping CEOs make better decisions and get ahead of the rapid growth of their competition.

> *The best way to be successful is to follow the advice you give others.*

The Woman of Inspiration

Mary Kay, founder of Mary Kay Cosmetics, a multi-billion dollar firm, says, *When I meet someone, I imagine her wearing an invisible sign that says, 'Make me feel important!' This is one of the most important lessons in dealing with people I have ever learned.*

I believe that each of us has God-given talents within us waiting to be brought into fruition. Every person is unique and special. It doesn't matter what you do for a living or how much money you have in the bank or how you look. People are people and everyone is important. I just try to look for the good qualities in everybody.

> **Work harder on improving yourself, than your job.**
> **Jim Rohn**

At appropriate times she shares her personal growth experience. When recovering from cancer chemotherapy treatment she shared, *As the Apostle Paul tells us in the Bible, he had a thorn in the flesh. He prayed many times to God to remove that thorn, but for whatever reason, He didn't choose to do so. But Paul continued to serve the Lord. I visualize my cancer as my thorn in the flesh.*

In time I began to realize that God was using me to reach other women. They saw how I endured my illness with courage, grit, and determination. In spite of the chemo, I had a high level of energy. I can't begin to tell you how many women have said to me, 'I was feeling sorry for myself because of my personal troubles, but then I look at you and I realized I had nothing to complain about. If you can do what you have done, I can overcome my problems.'

> **If our desires are to have the things of this world, they are never to be satisfied.**
> **Ben Franklin**

The Talent For Making Money

John D. Rockefeller's foundation has given over a billion dollars to various individuals and organizations for very significant causes. In his own mind, John D. was a steward of God's will.

He said, *I believe the power to make money is a gift from God — just as are the instincts for art, music, literature, the doctor's talent, and yours — to be developed and used to the best of our ability for the good of mankind. Having been endowed with the gift I possess, I believe it is my duty to make money and still more money and to use the money for the good of my fellowman according to the dictates of my conscience.*

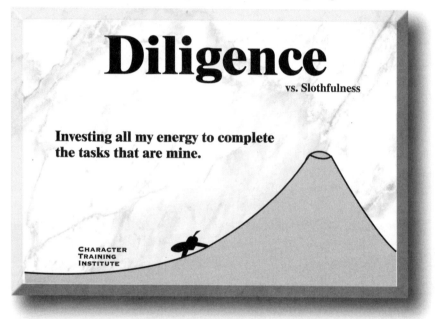

Diligence
vs. Slothfulness

Investing all my energy to complete the tasks that are mine.

CHARACTER TRAINING INSTITUTE

Service of the Master

The $3 billion public company with 200,000 employees, known as ServiceMaster, is a conglomerate of five different divisions serving hospitals, schools and homeowners. Their statement of business philosophy is:

- To honor God in all we do
- To help people develop
- To pursue excellence
- To grow profitably

Often ranked one of the most profitable companies in the USA, they consider their business concept of "stewardship" as the driving force of their business. James Heskett, a Harvard business school professor, has described ServiceMaster's approach as *a*

> *A man is rich according to what he is, not according to what he has.*

'quality wheel' in which employee development and satisfaction lead to high motivation, which leads to a higher level of service quality, which leads to a great customer satisfaction, which leads to increased volume and increased rewards, which further fuels employee satisfaction and ability to develop new people.

In his book, *The Soul of the Firm,* Bill Pollard, the current Chairman of ServiceMaster, says, *But profits for us is a means to a goal, not an end goal. What does it profit a man if he gains the whole world but loses his own soul? If we focus exclusively on profit, we would be a firm that had failed to nurture its soul. Eventually, I believe, firms that do this experience a loss in direction and purpose of their people, a loss in customers, and then a loss in profits.*

We make money at ServiceMaster. Our return on equity has averaged 50%. During the past twenty years, a share of our stock has grown in value from $1.00 per share to over $28.00 per share.

Sometimes the statement about God raises eyebrows, like this statement made by a shareholder, *While I firmly support the right of an individual to his religious convictions and pursuits, I totally fail to appreciate the concept that ServiceMaster is, in fact, a vehicle for the work of God. The multiple references to this effect, in my opinion, do not belong in any annual business report. To interpret a service for profit (which is what ServiceMaster does) as the work of God is an incredible presumption. Furthermore, to make a profit is not a sin. I urge that next year's business report be confined to just that — business.*

> *The mighty oak was once a little nut that stood its ground.*

Bill responded this way, *I believe there is a link. Profit is a means in*

God's world to be used and invested, not an end to be worshipped. *Profit is a legitimate measure of the value of our effort. It is an essential source of capital. It is a requirement for survival of the individual, the family unit, and any organization of society, whether it be a for profit company or not-for-profit organization. If you do not generate a surplus out of your annual operations, you will not generate a positive net worth. If you do not have a positive net worth, you will be operating in the red with a deficit. No organization, whether for-profit or not-for-profit, can survive with continuing deficit."*

In discussing their personal influence on the employees, Pollard makes this statement: *Some people may either question the existence of God or have different definitions for God. That is why at ServiceMaster we never allow religion or the lack thereof to become a basis for exclusion or how we treat each other professionally or personally. At the same time, I believe the work environment need not be emasculated to a neutrality of no belief.*

> **What we work for, we value most.**
>
> **Norman Vincent Peale**

The Game Plan

Joe Gibbs, former NFL Coach in the Hall of Fame, says, *The Bible is our game plan by God for the world. The world says you've got to make money, gain position and win football games. God says that is not it at all. He says if you have the right perspective of all those things, God is the key to those things.*

The only way to please the world is to win every time. Just read the newspapers; But that is not God's way. He loves us more when we have tough times than when we are winning.

The world says you only live one life — so live it until you die. The Bible says no, that your soul and spirit will live for ever. The question becomes where?

The Telescope

Clint Purvis, Chaplain for the Florida State football team, says *The Bible is a telescope...it brings God, His standards* and our life into focus. But to first move the dial on the telescope requires a commitment to Him...a commitment to become spiritual and open to His leading. Our author of life wants men and women who sincerely seek Him. Otherwise, we can peer through the telescope to see a book that seems fuzzy, historical, dull and of little sense.

The Bible is the key to spiritual growth. Just like our body needs food to grow or survive and the soul (or mind) needs an exchange of information to learn, the spirit needs the Word of God. Many times I feel the words penetrate my heart as I read His scripture.

ANYWAY

People are unreasonable, illogical, and self-centered,
Love them anyway.
If you do good, people will accuse you of ulterior motives,
Do good anyway.
If you are successful, you will win false friends
and true enemies,
Succeed anyway.
The good you do today, will be forgotten tomorrow,
Do good anyway.
Honesty and frankness makes you vulnerable,
Be honest and frank anyway.
People favor underdogs, but follow only top dogs,
Fight for some underdogs anyway.
What you spend years building may be destroyed overnight,
Build anyway.
People really need help,
but may attack you if you help them,
Help people anyway.
Give the world the best you've got,
you will get kicked in the teeth,
Give the world the best you've got anyway.

Dr. Robert Schuller

THE MORAL OF THE STORIES:

1. God is calling us to run our business and our life by His higher standards. The world's measure of success is touted as:

   (1)   money, wealth and size

   (2)   power and position

   (3)   possessions

   (4)   the social scene

   These are not God's priorities or ways of measuring us. His Book puts no emphasis on these things. His promises are spiritual, leading to peace, joy and a sense of fulfillment.   We can acquire some of the world's measure of success by His grace, inheritance, goals or circumstances and obeying His truths; but by themselves they will not buy love, peace or spiritual things which are more lasting. Life is eternal. We come into life naked as a little child and leave the same way.

2. Paraphrasing the Bible, *To whom much is given, much is required.* We are not all given the same talents or inheritance, but we are expected by God to maximize them, bringing a return on His investment in us. He loved us enough to bring us into the world and give us our talents. He is there to guide us and lead us all along the way, ready to give out many blessings. As one man put it, *Do your best, God will do the rest.*

3. When we exercise our talents, whether the result is fruitful or not, it becomes an experience of rich learning and character growth, which is pleasing to God.

4. He is working in our lives whether we recognize His hand or not. He will allow the consequences of our actions and the temptations of the world to confuse us, frustrate us or lead us into temporary joy. He allows us to go from Chicago to Dallas to Miami to get to Milwaukee (two steps forward and one step back). He wants us to take the route that builds our character by His standard and which opens the door for eternal success.

5. "Missing the mark" — Many people live life just working their God-given talents and doing their best to be a "moral" person. As a result, they may acquire money, possessions, respect and a good family but miss the real

> *True blessings are a results of the process of love – not achieving goals*

understanding of peace, love, joy and fulfillment with knowing Him in a spiritual relationship

What Do We Worship?

Laziness — is the lack of motivation from little or no faith in oneself or the true God. While it can relate to physical energy, it has more to do with the "grip" on the heart than the body or soul. It is an avoidance of pain, avoiding the fear of failure while interacting with other people. Sleep, TV, and food are ways to avoid reality and not have to deal with the fear inside. To God, it is waste of talent and love.

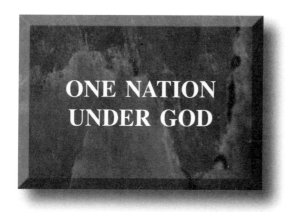

ONE NATION UNDER GOD

Character Truth: *Rule over every living creature.*

Character Quality: *Lead by example.*

Saved By America

Frederick Phillips is the retired CEO of Phillips Electronics, a $45 billion Dutch company he founded along with his father. During World War II, Frederick was put into a concentration camp for nearly three years by the German Gestapo. His wartime experience and appreciation leads him to make a powerful statement about the United States. He says, *America saved Europe four times. First, during World War I, then World War II, then with the Marshall Plan, and finally, saving us from nuclear destruction and the cold war.*

The First Freedom

President Ronald Reagan said, *I believe this blessed land was set apart in a very special way, a country created by men* and women who came here, not in search of gold, but in search of God. They would be free people, living under the law with faith in their Maker and their future.

The Pilgrims came to America to seek liberty, the pursuit of happiness, and the freedom to worship as they felt, not as the King dictated. It was a turbulent time when English kings thought nothing of persecuting people if they did not attend the church of state. Even the Pope thought during The Great Crusade there was nothing wrong with war and violence to acquire territories to spread or maintain his Christian gospel. The Pilgrims were the first European settlers in America and their pursuit of religious freedom became America's cornerstone and inspiration for other freedoms to follow.

Washington, The Man of Destiny

It may be rarely seen in history books, but George Washington fought for the British long before the American Declaration of Independence. As an officer for the British he was involved in an ambush by a tribe of Indians. While a number of officers' lives were lost, somehow Washington retreated with a small group, barely escaping with their lives. As he returned to the fort he discovered there were four bullet holes in his coat, but no blood or injury to his body. Many called it a miracle, and years later George Washington had an opportunity to meet the Indian Chief who led the massacre. He personally told Washington that he had shot at him seventeen times and that he wanted to meet this man who seemed to be "invincible." George Washington was protected by God for a greater destiny.

> *The person who knows something will always have a job. But those who know 'why' will always be his boss.*
>
> **Bob Harrison**

In recognition of the Pilgrims' contributions, one of George Washington's early official acts as the first President of the United States was the proclamation establishing Thanksgiving as a holiday. He wrote, *Whereas it is the duty of all nations to acknowledge the providence of*

Almighty God, to obey His will, to be grateful for His benefits, and to humbly implore His protection and favor. He went on later to call the nation to thankfulness to Almighty God.

CHARACTER QUALITY

- Lead by example -

Abraham Lincoln was a man of principles and character who, under great personal pressure, taxed his leadership ability to preserve our nation through the Civil War. The Battle of Gettysburg was a tragic time, but his words will forever be remembered.

Four score and seven years ago our fathers brought forth on this continent, a new nation, conceived in liberty, and dedicated to the proposition that all men are created equal.

He ended with these words, *We here highly resolve that these dead shall have not died in vain— that this nation, under God, shall have a new birth of freedom—and that the government of the people, by the people, for the people, shall not perish from the earth.*

Before 1776, there were no democracies. America's principles of freedom have been an inspiration to nearly half of the world's nations who have replicated parts of our model, including England and recently, former Communist countries.

It is self-evident that God has blessed America because of the faithfulness of its founders and believers. The key is whether other nations can grasp our spiritual and moral ethic, as well as our form of government.

The Conviction of Our Founders

Some of our skeptics and critics have wanted to disavow the research and proof that nearly all the founding fathers were Christians by their persuasion or convictions. They refer to them most notably as deists (a belief in God but also a belief that God would not interfere in the acts of men after his creation). At 81 years of age, during the Constitutional Convention, Benjamin Franklin made impassioned efforts to get the delegates to resolve their differences and get beyond the deadlocks that threatened the adoption of the Constitution. He said, *The small progress we have made after four or five weeks is melancholy proof of the imperfections of the human understanding.*

He reminded the delegates that during the War for Independence they had prayed regularly to God in that very hall: *Our prayers, sir, were heard, and they were graciously answered.*

Have we forgotten this powerful Friend, or do we imagine that we no longer need His assistance? I have lived, sir, a long time, and the longer I live, the more convincing proofs I see of this truth — that God governs in the affairs of men. And if a sparrow cannot fall to the ground without His notice, is it probable that an empire cannot rise without His aid? We have been assured, sir, in the sacred writings, that 'unless the Lord builds the house, its builders labor in vain.' I firmly believe this; and I also believe that without His concurring aid we shall succeed in this political building, no better than the builders of Babel. Franklin then suggested that daily prayers, led by one of Philadelphia's clergymen, be scheduled at the Convention.

> *He prefers to intervene in the affairs of men by invitation only.*

A Nation of Morals and Virtue

John Adams, the second President of the United States and one its outspoken founders, said in 1786, *Our Constitution is wholly inadequate for any nation but a religious and moral nation.*

Pope John Paul II said in a recent visit to the United States, that Americans should heed their founding fathers, *Every generation of Americans needs to know that freedom consists not in doing what we like, but in having the right to do what we ought. Democracy needs virtue, if it is not to turn against everything it is meant to defend and encourage. Democracy stands and falls with the truths and values which it embodies and promotes.*

Alexis de Toqueville, the noted French political philosopher of the nineteenth century, visited America in her infancy to find the secret of her greatness. As he traveled from town to town, he talked with people and asked questions. He examined our young national government, our schools, and centers of business, but could not find in them the reason for our strength. Not until he visited the churches of America and witnessed the pulpits of this land "aflame with righteousness" did he find the secret of our greatness. Returning to France, he summarized his findings*: America is great because America is good; and if America ever ceases to be good, America will cease to be great.*

Individual and business freedom requires self-discipline and respect for others, using the principles of morality.

Admitting The Obvious

Ted Koppel stated in a commencement speech given at Duke University, *In place of truth, we have discovered facts. For moral absolutes, we have substituted moral ambiguity. We now communicate with everyone and say absolutely nothing. We have reconstructed the Tower of Babel, and it is a television antenna. There have always been imperfect role models, false gods of material success and shallow fame. But now their influence is magnified by television.* He also stated that it is *The Ten Commandments, not the ten suggestions.*

> *Our weakness becomes strength when we depend upon Him to carry the heavy end.*

Biblical Roots

The New England Primer was published for children in the early American educational system by the colonists. It was a collection of Bible teachings pulled together in one book to teach reading. It had a great deal to do with teaching values and morals to young people for nearly a century, helping to build the American fiber.

David Barton of *Wallbuilders*, Aledo, Texas, discusses a University of Houston study which analyzed more than 15,000 political writings from 1760-1805: *The fact that the founders quoted the Bible more frequently than any other source, indisputedly makes it a significant commentary on its importance in the foundation of our government. 'Historians are discovering that the Bible, perhaps even more than the constitution is our founding document.'*

Inscribed on American money is the motto, *In God We Trust.* Similar quotes and Bible references are inscribed in or on the Capitol, Washington Monument, The Library of Congress, the Lincoln Memorial, Jefferson Memorial, and Dirkson Office Building. The Ten Commandments are inscribed above the head of the Chief Justice of the Supreme Court, and a prayer is said every day before sessions are begun in the House and Senate. There is little doubt that *God has shed His grace on thee,* even with all our failings and skepticism.

War, Prayer and Prosperity

World War II may have been the greatest time in the growth of America's character. Prayer was the key. Americans in the U.S. were praying for the soldiers abroad; the soldiers abroad were praying for their families at home and the war effort. Great sacrifices were made. Ethnic prejudices and national origins were set aside. Americans were brought closer together fighting enemies on both sides of the world, with a national reliance on God.

Historians say the Normandy invasion could not have been accomplished without its surprise elements facilitated by the right weather (after it had been postponed two days) that produced a fog to cover the amphibious landing of troops that surprised the Germans. Eisenhower called it the Great Crusade and the code words for mission accomplished were *Praise the Lord.*

The 1950s may have been the greatest time of prosperity and tranquillity in America's history. Many say it was not because of our own great intelligence, might and determination, but because of a loving God who blessed us for our faithful and righteous acts of sacrifice.

Americans remained in a "state of thanksgiving" after World War II because their prayers had been answered. It was considered the greatest time of economic prosperity and tranquillity in America. War, tragedy, and catastrophe brings greater numbers to prayer than any other events.

There were other wars and political movements that had a significant impact on America's character and spirit, i.e., the Civil War and the Civil Rights Movement. Amazingly, Sadam Hussein declared during the Gulf War that his god would lead him to victory over America. Even our news media was urging Americans to say a prayer for our soldiers. Unbeknownst to most of us, the military took 50,000 body bags to the Middle East in preparation for the worst. The casualties did not exceed 300. Was that because of our great military might, technology, planning and strategy? Faith says there was a higher power leading us to do what was right.

America is God's second Noah's Ark

Economic Leader

When examining world history, how could a nation in just 150 years become the greatest economic power the world has ever seen? Was it because we were smarter? Had more diverse people with great talent? Had more resources? Or a great educational system? Or was it because we had the right principles from founders who sought the right God, using the right manual for success?

OUR FATHER IN HEAVEN:

WE PRAY that YOU save us from *ourselves*.

The world that YOU have made for us, to live in peace,
we have made into an armed camp.
We live in fear of war to come.

We are afraid of "the terror that flies by
night, and the arrow that flies by day
the pestilence that walks in darkness
and the destruction that wastes at noon-day."

We have turned from YOU to go our selfish way
We have broken YOUR commandments
and denied YOUR truth. We have left YOUR altars
to serve the false gods of money and pleasure and power.

FORGIVE US AND HELP US

Now, darkness gathers around us and we are confused
in all our counsels. Losing faith in YOU,
we lose faith in ourselves.

Inspire us with wisdom, all of us of every color, race and creed,
to use our wealth, our strength to help our brother,
instead of destroying him.

Help us to do YOUR will as it is done in heaven
and to be worthy of YOUR promise of peace on earth.

Fill us with new faith, new strength and new courage,
that we may win the Battle for Peace.

Be swift to save us, *dear GOD,*
before the darkness falls ★☆★

★☆★FROM "THE BATTLE FOR PEACE" AN ADDRESS BY CONRAD N. HILTON
A PUBLIC SERVICE MESSAGE BY CONRAD N. HILTON, PRESIDENT, HILTON HOTELS CORPORATION
REPRINTED FROM A 1952 ADVERTISEMENT REPRINTED WITH PERMISSION

AMERICA ON ITS KNEES:

☆ ☆ ☆ *not beaten there by the hammer & sickle, but* FREELY, INTELLIGENTLY, RESPONSIBLY, CONFIDENTLY, POWERFULLY. *America now knows it can destroy* communism & *win the battle for* peace. We need fear nothing *or no one...* ...except *GOD.*

Conrad Hilton, founder of Hilton Hotels, was touched and profoundly moved by the need to make Americans aware of the deeply vital role played by the freedom of religion, a right given by God, in its fight for political freedom.

In 1952, he wrote this prayer, published in the *Saturday Evening Post* and other publications on July 4. America's heart was grateful to God for the end of World War II, but the tension from communism was high, and the Korean Conflict brought new fears. There was a need for strong convicted men to stand firm in their faith. America needed Conrad Hilton's words of purpose, encouragement and new resolve during this trying period. Over 300,000 people wrote letters of support to Conrad and asked for copies of the prayer.

PAINTED BY TEXANA

Conrad M Hilton

PRESIDENT HILTON HOTELS CORPORATION

World Missions

The Bible says, *Give and it will be given unto you*. The tongue-in-cheek joke often quoted around the world is, *If you want to build yourself into a great economic power, you should first have a war with the United States; lose, and they will give you all the money you need to start over and teach you how to do it*. In addition to the money our country gives to nations around the world, 90% of the world's mission giving for spreading the gospel comes from Americans.

Some might say, if the principles of a Judeo-Christian faith drive the system of America's economic might, then how can

RIGHTS FROM THE CREATOR

Newt Gingrich, after studying the Federalist Papers, shared the perception that the Founding Fathers believed that man's rights came from God, not a king. They believed that God had granted man free will to choose and form a government by His standards, rather than the standards dictated by a king or monarch who decided by his personal will the fate of a nation's people.

Note from the Declaration of Independence: *When in the course of human events, it becomes necessary for one people to dissolve the political bonds . . . to assume among the powers of the earth . . . to which the Law of Nature and of Nation's God entitle them . . . We hold these truths to be self-evident, that all men are created equal, that they are endowed by their Creator with certain inalienable Rights, that among these are Life, Liberty, and the Pursuit of Happiness.*

They believed that government came from the rights of people, given by God, rather than by an authority having the right to push the government down and onto people. Communism is based on the teaching that there is no God; the State has the final word in all matters. Unfortunately, decisions then return to the whim of leaders and their self-serving motives.

Japan have become such a great economic success? Before World War II, Japan was ruled by the military and a monarchy. The war humbled the Japanese. After the Japanese defeat, the Americans trained them in the principles; *Love your customers, employees, and neighbor as yourself*, (the Golden Rule), taught them ethics based on God's moral truths, limited their military, got them into the automobile industry, taught them to build high-quality products, set up their government and free enterprise system, gave them the money, and bought their products. Yes, the Japanese combined this with their intelligence, hard work, and aggressiveness—all part of His truths.

Germany was also humbled and returned to its Christian heritage and principles and used American financial and management assistance to regain its strength by focusing on The Golden Rule. In most military victories, the saying is, *to the winner go the spoils*. But in the case of the American victory over Germany, the result was the Marshall Plan—according to many people, the greatest act of human kindness in history.

Four Significant Deterrents

There is a drawing away from Biblical truths in our society. There are a number of events and circumstances that have seriously detracted from America's resolve, convictions, and principles, such as:

1. The 1963 decision by the Supreme Court to ban school prayer. Since that time serious violent crime has increased by 500%, divorces have more than doubled, values have deteriorated, and SAT scores remain the same or declined.

2. With good intentions, many entitlement and welfare programs have deflated the human spirit of many of our citizens. Creativity and initiative are literally desensitized. People become controlled by a system. Their freedoms are limited and they look to the government for their answers rather than turning to God, having faith in themselves and using self-determination to resolve their own needs!

3. False perceptions are created by the media and communication industry. Local reporters monitoring police reports emphasize crime over the good accomplished by 98% of the population. Crime reports are used as lead

stories on TV news shows, in the hope of shocking viewers into watching their coverage. They create the image that morals are not important and have no bearing or consequences on society.

4. Finally, we have the increasing threat of too many lawyers (we have 70% of the world's lawyers, 94% of the lawsuits and only 6% of the population) seeking cases and chasing high ticket judgments no matter what the scruples of their clients. Unfortunately some seek greed and power, rather than integrity. Their mission seems to be to find the loopholes in the law. As John Adams noted, the American Constitution was written for a nation of moral people, doing what is right.

> *We have staked the whole future of American civilization not upon the power of government, far from it. We have staked the future of all of our political institutions upon the capacity of each and all of us to govern ourselves according to the Ten commandments of God.*
>
> **James Madison**

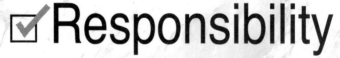

Knowing and doing what is expected of me

☑ Responsibility

CHARACTER TRAINING INSTITUTE

vs. Unreliability

THE MORAL OF THE STORIES:

1. America, with all its faults, is God's best hope and example for the world because of its founders and believers who today work toward modeling His character.

2. It's a myth that separation of church and state is part of our Constitution. America's forefathers intended that the government would not establish a single denomination as the official church of the government of the United States (as done in England). Their intent was freedom of choice, not keep religious teaching out of government or schools.

3. He wants nations where freedom and the ability to witness can exist without retribution. He is the founder of the principle of freedom, free will in life—the choice to believe or not.

4. While surveys indicate that anywhere between 33-46% of Americans are committed Christians, are many of us blessed and protected because of their prayers? Or is it because of the commitment of our founders and the generations of blessings God promises in scripture? Or both?

5. The secrets to continued economic success are dependent on the proper application of God's truths. America is more successful than other nations because it uses them more often. Yet, its potential is far from being realized.

6. The reason why eleven Presidents and Congresses since 1950 have so strongly defended the rights of Israel is not because the Israelis are always right but because He is working through the hearts of Americans to protect our Judeo-Christian heritage for a greater plan yet to come.

7. Why have lower SAT scores and so many other negative consequences occurred since the 1963 act by the Supreme Court of removing prayer from school? When we fail to respect and live by His truths, the consequences are negative in the long term.

8. The Spirit of our founders provided new individual and corporate freedoms never before granted in the world. They require moral people who believe, and seek Him, not big government, for their answers.

9. The Spirit of our ancestors lives in our nation through the truths they discovered, which guide our paths.

Bible Influence on American Culture

Biblical Truths	Examples of Laws, Ethics, Traditions & Programs
• God gave man Free Will.	Emphasis on individual freedoms: religion, speech, the press, commerce, taking of individual initiative and risk, and the pursuit of personal potential; and democracy.

Character Truths

• Take on God's image.	American motto, *In God We Trust* Founding fathers focused on character of people.
• Be fruitful and increase.	Focus on faith, risk and growth of the individual, family, organizations and nation; acceptance of change, having faith about good things to come. (Trust in God.)
• Fill the earth and subdue it.	Use of talents to please God; belief in the Protestant work ethic.
• Rule over every living creature.	Establishment of government by the people, for the people, and elected to serve the people. Emphasis on individual rights: life, liberty and pursuit of happiness.

Spiritual Truths

• **Love God**	**Seek His Direction**
• Have no other Gods before Me.	Freedom of Religion, reflected in holidays celebrated: Christmas, Hanukkah, Thanksgiving, Easter, Prayer, Singing, e.g. *God Bless America.*
• Have no false idols.	Laws concerning self harm, drug addiction, drunk driving, rape, harm to others, adultery.
• Do not use God's name in vain	Self-censorship in media; restraint & good taste. Sayings, e.g. *Thank God, Lord Willing, God Bless You* as people sneeze.

Biblical Truths	Examples of Laws, Ethics, Traditions & Programs
• Keep the Sabbath Holy.	Study, learn and grow spiritually. Most businesses close on Sunday, and nearly half of Americans attend church and spend time with their family.

Moral Truths

• **Love your neighbor as yourself.**	**Serve your customers, employees, and friends. American business ethics are based on Moral Biblical truths.**
• Honor your father and mother.	Respect is shown to elders; Father's Day and Mother's Day reflect this, as do Social Security, Medicare, Senior Citizen age discounts.
• Do not murder.	The criminal justice and legal systems to put offenders in jail or in prison.
• Do not commit adultery.	Marriage and divorce laws: marriages are a public covenant with God. Business ethics and policies promote loyalty to customers and employees; sexual harassment laws.
• Do not steal.	Rights of private property and the legal system enforcement. Business ethics, e.g. Copyright laws, offering forgiveness after sentences are served. This truth motivates volunterism and giving to others by individuals, churches, businesses, philanthropy.
• Do not bear false witness.	Business ethics stress, recognize and reward honesty. Swearing in, in court or for a new office, on a Bible, saying, *So help me God*, also the expression, *Honest to God Truth*.
• Do not covet.	Rights of private property, civil rights legislation and enforcement reflect this truth, giving to appreciate others, e.g. food banks.

Moral Truths

The last six truths of the Ten Commandments are guidelines for loving our fellowman. The Lord embodied them when He said to *Love your neighbor as yourself*. This is also known as the Golden Rule—*Do unto others as you would have them do unto you*.

These truths have become the most widely accepted foundations for business ethics in America, with growing acceptance throughout the world.

As businesses and individuals continue to learn ways to love (caring, showing empathy, listening and serving), their neighbors (employees, customers, suppliers, vendors, community and stockholders) and use their God given Character Truths according to His will, they shall become more richly blessed.

Being *customer focused* was His design long before the CEOs, business authors, consultants and professors discovered it as the central way to succeed in business.

WE ARE FAMILY BY DESIGN

Moral Truth: *Honor your father and mother.*

Character Quality: *Respect authority as family.*

Family Values

James Cash Penney, a mentor to many executives in and out of his own company, enjoyed sharing the story of how, as a young man, he lived on a farm in Missouri. His father struggled in farming and also served as the unpaid pastor of the local church. One day his father asked the elders of the church if they would consider paying him for his time and services. The elders called a meeting with an open discussion that Jim and his mother witnessed, as his father explained his need. Many elders were upset, because a pastor had never been paid in their church before. They voted against his father's request and asked him to resign.

Afterward his father never wavered in his faith, held a grudge or expressed bitterness and resentment. That example taught Jim a great lesson that influenced his entire life. He would take *The Golden Rule*, as his father taught him, to its full intent—*Put the customers' needs first and maintain a forgiving attitude should they not be satisfied*.

After his great business success, Jim Penney built a retirement home for pastors in North Florida in memory of his father and mother. It is still in operation today. He never forgot the example and truths his mother and father taught him.

Jim Penney told executives that he believed that the best course for business is the *Sermon on the Mount* found in the Book of Matthew. *If we just follow the principles of Christ we will win the loyalty of our customer, go the second mile, give and it will be given back to us, and we will serve well. In the long run we will win many friends.*

The Business Family

Norm Miller is CEO of Interstate Batteries, a $500 million company based in Dallas, Texas. He selected Jim Coté to be his Chaplain and created a department to offer spiritual counseling, not only to the employees, but also to distributors and their families as part of the Interstate greater organization.

Jim believes that *the CEOs of today are the bishops of tomorrow.* His company department distributes 200,000 newsletters a year, provides a complete library of books and reference materials for family and personal issues, leads Bible Studies on request and does individual counseling in person or by phone. More recently they developed a whole video counseling series entitled *Marriage and the Road* for couples in which one or both spouses are gone from the home for extended periods of time.

> *We have to undo a hundred-year-old concept and convince our managers that their role is not to control people and stay 'on top of them,' but rather to guide, energize and excite.*
>
> **Jack Welch, CEO, General Electric**

More and more companies are moving to the chaplain concept as they help their employees deal with personal or family issues, because they impact work and their character. The company employs the whole person with all their emotions, both good and bad. Marketplace Ministries of Dallas works with over 175 companies, furnishing chaplains for counseling, hospital visits, and marriage counseling, and also providing many other services to their employees and families.

CHARACTER QUALITY

- Respect Authority As Family -

The Lord chose a father and mother to create a family unit for the conception and nurturing of each of us. The roots of our values come from our family. The family gives us our name and heritage. It represents those in authority above us who are to be respected. The family is our emotional stronghold where we must learn to forgive, become good stewards and eventually become better and more loving parents ourselves.

Businesses are an extended family for employees, especially for those who come from broken homes and who never learned the basic values He intended. Employees who have had problems with their parents and failed to learn respect for authority bring the same attitude into the work environment. Every business teaches truth or values. The question is whether they also "walk their talk." What eternal truths does your business teach? Since every life is eternal, how we respect and influence our families can live forever.

Father's Inspiration

The legendary film maker, Cecil B. deMille, says it was his father's influence that inspired him to go into the motion picture industry. *We had to agree to rub his head so that he would read us Old Testament Bible stories before we went to* bed. *He became so soothed and relaxed that he would forget the hour and go on reading extra chapters to us as we sat intently around his chair.*

I have no doubt that my father's vivid reading planted in my impressionable mind a reverence and respect for the Bible, perhaps even a sense of dramatic values which in subsequent years was to turn me to the Great Book for themes to thrill motion picture audiences.

Cecil said that he had always been aware that the Bible was the perpetual "best seller" of all books, so he produced the movies *The Ten Commandments, The King of Kings, The Sign of the Cross,* and *The Crusades.* He once said, *I've been in Hollywood since 1913, during which time actors, actresses, directors and producers have passed in seemingly endless procession, some befriended by destiny, others lost in oblivion. In a maelstrom like Hollywood there are many reasons for failure and unhappiness. I believe the chief among these is the failure to realize that the purpose of this life is understanding of the spirit and not worship before the calf of gold.* It is too bad that Cecil isn't around today to tell some of our present movie producers his story.

Love Has Different Degrees

Sensual: physical attraction, touch, look, smell, sexual desire.

Respectful: authority, want to serve, seeking recognition.

Emotional: feelings, caring, sensitivity.

Rational: decision to, ought to, want to, desire to...

Agape: God's spirit flowing through a person, the strongest and most pure love, and as stated in I Corinthians 13:4.

Family First

Mary Kay says, *Our company was founded on our belief in The Golden Rule. We believe in treating people fairly, as we want to be treated ourselves. We apply this basic belief to every decision we make.*

> ***Put others before yourself, and you can become a leader among men.***

In accordance with The Golden Rule, we strive to provide opportunities for women to achieve their maximum potential. We tell all of our consultants and directors that God and their family come before our company — and whenever they experience a conflict, the company should be put in third place.

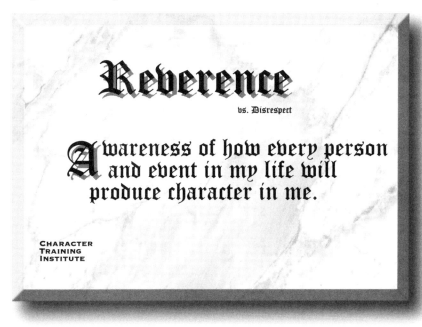

Reverence

vs. Disrespect

Awareness of how every person and event in my life will produce character in me.

CHARACTER
TRAINING
INSTITUTE

Returning Respect

When it was time for me to step down from the day-to-day operations from the company I built from bankruptcy to $150 million in sales, says Jim Miller, CEO of BT Office Products, *I refused to sell just to the highest bidder who would typically cut a third of our people and overhead so we became an instant*

> *America was founded on faith, so businesses had enough faith to take risks. Ongoing success is a result of using His principles.*

plus to their bottom line. My people have respected my authority and leadership for all these years and I owe them something in return so I sold a third of my stock to them at a very reasonable price and no one lost a job. Yet our way of doing business keeps doing better. Our customer satisfaction index of 99.67 is a verification of that.

Biblical Inspiration

Samsonite Corporation was founded in 1910 by Jessie Shwayder with his life savings of $3,500 and a firm conviction to The Golden Rule. *Do unto others as you would have them do unto you was the only way to do business,* says Jessie, who felt that strong luggage—luggage as strong as Samson in the Bible—was his key advantage over the competition. Samson was what he initially named his products, but later it was changed to Samsonite. Each new employee was given a marble plaque with a reminder of The Golden Rule.

Jessie believed God had entrusted him with the talents, resources, vision and capability to produce such a product, so he wanted to honor *His Heavenly Father* by sharing his principles with his employees, customers and suppliers.

Family Blessing

In 1979, Julius Erving, the famous NBA basketball player, sustained an injury that kept him out half the season. He said *Somehow I got a chance to put things in perspective. We had a family reunion of 300 people on a three day weekend. We traced our history and I learned of a strong Christian influence, which I had not known before. One uncle told me that two generations before I was born my family put a blessing on me. They asked the Lord to bless me.*

I had to pursue this. As my uncle counseled me he said he had always been praying for me. His counsel put things in perspective and I was touched. I consecrated a relationship with Christ and it brought peace to my life and a destiny I had not known. It brought our family together to understand our purposes.

> *The best way to forget your own problems is to help someone solve his.*

Father's Love

As Richard Kughn plodded home one day from school he found a cast-off Lionel train engine. He took it home and later that night showed it to his dad. His dad took it apart and cleaned it and showed his son how it was put together. That was the beginning of a lasting relationship which influenced his life.

He claimed his dad had a God-given understanding of how to treat him with respect and to develop a relationship that through the years went beyond father and son, becoming more like partners. He grew up, graduated from college, and was employed by a major corporation before leaving to start his own company. After a number of years of success he attended a train collectors show. A friend said, *Dick, why don't you buy the Lionel Toy Train Company? I heard the company was for sale.* He laughed and dismissed the idea, but he couldn't get it out of his mind. After months of study his friends and associates advised him not to buy the company; but as he prayed and pondered his decision, he knew that God could see far deeper into things than he could.

In listening for direction, and seeking the Lord's guidance, I thought of dad and me and what assembling and operating my train had meant to us. Soon after that I came across a picture of an old Lionel ad. It showed a youngster and his father on their knees amid a train layout, with the legend, 'Keep young with your boy and he will grow older with you.'

That picture made me think of the wide gap that seems to exist between children and parents nowadays. So I bought the company.

Over Ninety

Tony Campolo refers to a survey he conducted of people over 90 years old who were asked what three things might they do differently if they could live their life over again. These are the three answers that were most common:

1. Take more risks—be open, let other people in.
2. Reflect more— avoid saying, *just as soon as I get this done.*
3. Do things that are eternal —things that live on beyond earth.

This is sound advice for all of us under the age of 90. Before it is too late to influence others, or thank a boss, or counsel with an employee, we need to focus on the truths that bring each of us in tune with His eternal purpose of mutual respect and honor.

THE MORAL OF THE STORIES:

1. Honor those who brought you here, whether they have loved you or not. God has a purpose for everyone he has placed in our paths and lives. Our role is to love one another, to be forgiving and not hold on to bitterness and resentment. Seeking His love can help us overcome the past and bring back the sweet memories of the best of times for eternity.

2. Look to your employers with respect and honor, even if they have not treated you the way you would like. Pray for them. Share with them and be a part of each others' extended family.

3. Be a better parent. Spend time, share your values, get into the Bible and fellowship with your spouse, kids and parents. Our purpose in family life is relationships, not toys or big accomplishments.

4. Share with your employees and peers life-changing and eternal truths. They may never get them anywhere else.

5. Show respect to father, mother or boss. Surprise them with a recognition event. Remind them of their outstanding qualities, contributions and appreciate results.

6. Pray for everyone in authority over you. Learn to love them.

7. The number one place where character and truth are taught (or fail to be taught) is in the home by parents. The family is the cornerstone for the direction of our society. Day care can't teach the same values that mom and dad can.

Business Success

The greatest factor in the ongoing success of business and careers is the ability of the executives and employees to follow the character and moral truths of The Ten Commandments (also known as The Golden Rule) in their effort to "love" (show care, empathy, service, and fulfilling the needs) of employees, customers, suppliers, vendors, community, and finally (not first) stockholders.

You ask, how then can "sin" businesses such as pornography publishers, drug dealers, and alcohol companies be successful? These companies also do their best to try to love or entice their potential customers who seek to quench the hurt in their heart. God loves the sinner (we all are sinners) but hates the sin. He provides grace to all for a period of time. God is hoping the sinner will turn from his evil ways before he leaves the earth.

Movement To And From His Truths

Focus:

Others
⇧
Love
⇧
Faith
⇧
Him

Consequences:

Blessings
⇧
Purpose
⇧
Joy
⇧
Peace

Seeking The Higher Purpose

You sense blessings, peace
You are an example for others
Higher levels of performance
Sense of teamwork, family, realize goals
Both parties listen
Lines of communication open
Appreciation leads to love, promotion
Mutual respect grows
Express gratitude
Thankfulness for parents, employees

Moral Truth: Honor Father and Mother

Holding resentment toward authority
Cooperate minimally
Being ungrateful
Talk behind friends' backs
Get back at them
No forgiveness
Resentment turned to bitterness
Self pity, bad attitude, jealousy
Divorce, resignation, firing

Focus:

Self
⇩
Negatives
⇩
Works
⇩
Fear

Consequences:

Unrestful
⇩
Stress
⇩
Pain
⇩
Sickness

Falling To Deeper Depths

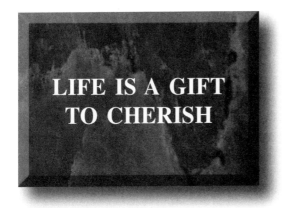

LIFE IS A GIFT TO CHERISH

Moral Truth: *Do not murder.*

Character Quality: *Forgive and value life.*

Hate or Forgiveness?

Adolph Coors, IV, faced what is probably the greatest tragedy that any of us can face, especially at the young age of 14 years. His father, who ran the Colorado brewery founded by his great grandfather, was kidnapped and murdered—shot several times in the back. His body was found seven months later near Denver.

Adolph's mother never recovered from the experience. For seventeen years Adolph lived with hate, anger and resentment for the man who murdered his father; his life was a series of events that ended in frustration. The burden of caring for the family name and living up to unrealistic expectations was very heavy, and he spent only a limited time in the family business.

One day his life changed dramatically. Adolph became a committed Christian. Total love and peace flooded him. He cried like a baby; all of the pain and hurt trapped inside of him seemed to rush out with tears.

His life changed as he grew in his Christian walk, yet one burden seemed still to be there—the resentment toward the man who murdered his father. Through the persistent urging of a friend he visited the prison where the man was incarcerated.

His father's killer refused to see him. So he wrote him a letter saying, *I ask for your forgiveness for the hatred I have had for you for seventeen years and I forgive you for what you have done to me and my family.* He visited twice more but never was face-to-face with his father's murderer.

However, on the last trip another inmate spoke with him and said, *He got the letter, and it touched him. Your letter has also gone from cell to cell throughout the entire prison. You will never realize how great an impact this has had on the prisoners here, Mr. Coors.*

The Golden Rule

I live by the Golden Rule, says Jim Moran, founder of Southeast Toyota, one of the largest automobile distributors in the world. *I don't think respect or courtesy or kindness should be based on how much money a person has or what they can do for me. It does not matter whether you are the biggest customer or take out the trash — you deserve to be treated the way I want you to treat me.* Jim has had many colorful business experiences and attributes his success to living by the Golden Rule.

> *The cure for crime is not in the electric chair, but in the high chair.*

Two Legends From the Same Branch

Jim Penney was a real pioneer in 1905. He broke away from the business practice of "gouging", commonly practiced in the "wild west" mining towns. His *Penney Idea* set a new standard, still emulated today by many businesses. He was

CHARACTER QUALITY

- Forgive And Value Life -

Unforgiveness hurts the person carrying the resentment far more than the person to whom the bitterness is directed. This is why Jesus said to *love your enemy*. According to God's design our heart can be severely damaged by unforgiveness, which in time can create sickness or even death. Man deceives himself with the notion of getting revenge. God is the final judge in all matters. Forgiveness is not an option. Our job is to focus on the central point of His truths which are about relationships—how to create a loving relationship with Him and our fellowman, and how to have self-discipline, respect, and consideration for one another. This is what pleases Him. At the same time, He wants to help us accomplish His purposes.

Business is not primarily about money, profits, stockholders, equity, return on investment or even whether we pay someone at or above the industry average. These things are secondary.

God's measuring stick is spiritual. How much love, respect, dignity, empathy, and fairness do we share with our employees, family, friends and even adversaries. He did not create any "junk", but we all have handicaps —God made us that way on purpose, so that need Him.

It is not our job to allow negative emotions to create disrespect between us. He has already forgiven us and paid the price. The least we can do is to forgive those who offend us, and treat them with respect. Second to the family unit, business has the biggest obligations to fulfill His plan, *walking the truth* and being His example. *Vengeance is mine* says the Lord. After the law of the land, God will punish those who fail to repent. Besides the family unit, business has the biggest obligations to fulfill His plan, *walking the truth* and being His example.

the first to call employees associates, to share a third of the profits with the managers who were called partners, to price goods fairly rather than gouging, to focus on customers' satisfaction, to train associates, and to help men and women develop their character.

Even though Sam Walton, founder of Wal-Mart, only worked for the J. C. Penney Company for a short time, he was fascinated with the *Penney Idea*. Sam was a master at learning from successful companies, but his frugal and conservative nature kept him from sharing company profits for many years. He later shared this in his book:

In the early days, we paid as little as we could get by with. The larger truth I failed to see was, the more you share profits with associates (employee salary, incentives, stock), the more profits will accrue to the company. Why? Because the managers

THE PENNEY IDEA

To serve the public, as nearly as we can, to its complete satisfaction.

To expect for the service we render a fair remuneration and not all the profit the traffic will bear.

To do all in our power to pack the customer's dollar full of value, quality and satisfaction.

To continue to train ourselves and our associates so that the service we give will be more and more intelligently performed.

To improve constantly the human factor in our business.

To reward men and women in our organization through participation in what the business produces.

To test our every policy, method and act in this wise: "Does it square with what is right and just?"

treat associates in the way the associates will treat the customer— and if the associates treat customers well they will come back over and over, and over and that is where the real profit lies, not in dragging first time strangers into the store for a one time purchase based upon splashy sales or expensive advertising.

Listen To Me

The late Maurice Mascarenhas, enthusiastic Strategic Planning consultant, shared this true story many times. Concerned about quality and competitiveness a very large company decided that it needed to get more employee involvement and set up a "suggestion system" to gather, review, implement and reward employees for their concepts which would save the company money and improve productivity. All the top executives seemed to be pretty proud of the system as it started to work.

A year later at a dinner to recognize employees and give them cash bonuses, a long-time hourly employee by the name of Herb Johnson was recognized. Herb's suggestion had saved the company nearly half a million dollars and the CEO was proud to give him a check for $5,000. Herb was asked to make a comment.

He said, *I'm honored to receive this award and very pleased that the company had decided to recognize me for this contribution. I have been with the company for 14 years and made this same suggestion to my supervisor 12 years ago. He told me to button my lip, get to work and stop*

> *Listening shows interest, respect and love, like the healing power of a prayer.*

being so critical. All these years you have had my hands and now there may be hope that you will also get my heart and soul, as well.

Bring Your Problems

Tom Watson and his son were credited for the significant growth and development of IBM over many years. He continually visited factories and spent hours talking with workers, inspiring the concept of *Management By Walking Around*. Many of them considered him their friend rather than the CEO.

One day an employee flew from Endicott to New York to see Watson. Doctors had told him that a younger brother had an incurable disease and would not live long. The distressed employee thought maybe Watson could do something beyond the medical resources of a small community. Within hours, the patient was under the care of a famous specialist in a top hospital, relieving his brother's anxiety. The employee tried to apologize for perhaps over-stepping his bounds, but Watson interrupted him, When he said *bring your problems to me, I meant exactly that.*

> *You cannot live a perfect day without doing something for someone who will never be able to repay you.*
>
> **John Wooden**

Policy Manuals

Robert Townsend, former President of Avis Rent-a-Car, in his updated book, *Further Up the Organization,* advocates: *Don't bother with policy manuals. If they are general, they are useless. If they are specific, they are how-to manuals — expensive to prepare and revise. If you have to have a policy manual, publish The Ten Commandments.*

The Right Goal

As a partner in the New York City office of Ernst and Whinney, an international CPA firm, Homer Figler personally committed to his pastor that he would read the Bible at least 15 minutes a day. The more he read, the more it seemed to change his life and perspective on things. Besides experiencing a personal impact, he could see how it directly affected business also. For example, he shared, *One time I was having difficulty illustrating the importance of goal setting to a group of men and my Bible reading came to my rescue. I was able to show these executives an example of what happened to some people who were also working on a major project, people who did everything right except for one important element.*

Indeed, the ancient people described in the first nine verses of Genesis 11 had a common goal: to build a great city with a tower reaching to Heaven. They were in complete unity on the method, using fire-hardened bricks for permanence. They committed themselves whole-heartedly to the task. But one thing was wrong—their goal. In effect, they were building the tower as a monument to themselves, putting themselves on a level with God. As a result, the tower was destroyed.

If a goal — corporate, family or personal — is not morally right, something somewhere along the line is bound to break down. If a project is not fair to all those concerned, then those involved tend to let their private desires get in the way of the common goal. Communication breaks down, mistrust builds and instead of working together as a team, the group scatters — like the builders of the tower of Babel.

A Short Course In Human Relations

The SIX most important words:
I admit I made a mistake

The FIVE most important words:
You did a good job

The FOUR most important words:
What is your opinion?

The THREE most important words:
If you please

The TWO most important words:
Thank you or Forgive me

The ONE most important word:
We

The LEAST most important word:
I

My Father

When Wes Cantrell, CEO of Lanier Worldwide, was growing up in Hiram, Georgia, his father was pastor of a local church. The church had a policy of annually rehiring its pastor.

One year, as Wes, his father and family drove up to the church for the annual business meeting, something was obviously different than expected. The parking lot was full of cars, and normally only fifteen or twenty cars would be at such a meeting.

When they went in, the church was full. Most of the people there seldom came on Sunday. It seems a group of men had organized the vote to terminate his dad as pastor.

Wes' natural reaction was to be angry or bitter. His father was a good man, he preached well, and was true to the Word. Wes could not understand why or how a church could treat him so cruelly.

Over time his family had to deal with this situation. Surprisingly for Wes, his father dealt with it extremely well. If he harbored any bitterness toward the ringleaders, those who led the charge to get him out, it was never apparent.

But, at fifteen, Wes questioned even going to church. He literally wrote off the church as having no value. Yet his father did something that was quite remarkable. He went back to that church and taught a Sunday School class. His act of forgiveness was quite a lesson for Wes. He said, *I might not be active in the church or gone on with my Christian life had it not been for my father's act of total humility.*

Even today, that church bears some of the scars of that event, but in my family, the potential anger and bitterness that could have resulted are replaced with empathy and love. My father died in 1971. Nevertheless, I will always remember this and other great attributes of his life, and how he influenced me. No other man has had a greater impact on my life—he taught me about true forgiveness, which has greatly influenced my personal life and business career.

Unforgiveness will torment you. If you don't forgive, you can't be forgiven.

84

Divine Listening

After Jack Stack, CEO of Springfield Remanufacturing (SRC), and his team of executives were able to raise the capital to buy their company, they got production into high gear with a new sales effort. Jack felt pretty comfortable about their new direction. Things seemed

> *The heart is the happiest when it beats for others.*

to be running on all cylinders. Then one day walking down the hall he noticed a young man sweeping and said hello to him. The young man said, *Did you know that 76% of our receivables are in trucking and every seven years the industry goes down? If the economy ever turns down, we will have problems.* I said, 'Thank you, Lord.'

It just so happened that this young man had been a burned-out stockbroker and out of the pressure of it all decided to take a break and work for us. I was so taken by his comment and realized that he was 'right on' and went back to our management team and said, 'Do you realize that if we have an economic downturn we will be in trouble?'

It was the turning point for SRC to diversify their business. Jack later said, *That was a profound statement for our business and really changed the direction of our firm. I'm not sure everyone believes in divine intervention, but I do.*

Open Book Principles

American business executives seem to be constantly looking for the next "fix" or management trend that will be the answer for the continual improvement and success in their business. Obviously the concepts of Empowerment, TQM, Re-Engineering, Value Added and Self-Directed Work Teams, plus many other business concepts, will continue to help the organizations be more effective and efficient. With the right motives and aligned with God's truths, businesses that follow these ethical practices will be blessed. The *Open Book Management* concept, made famous by Jack Stack and his team, can help businesses come even closer to adhering to the moral truths of The Ten Commandments if companies are willing to take the risks to implement them and *walk their talk.*

Open Book Management focuses on four basic principles:

1. Sharing information and knowledge with everyone.
2. Teaching business literacy to everyone.
3. Sharing a stake in the outcomes with everyone.
4. Creating a company of entrepreneurs.

Open Book Management succeeds because it encompasses trust, relationships, and team accomplishments. It allows risks, treats people as family, and creates open communication. Integrity and honesty form square one. I believe it reduces jealousy, internal competition, egotism, and the spread of rumors; it heightens morale. Overall, it creates a better company culture. Business needs to be both fun and profitable for all, and OBM can do this, if led by top executives with loving motives. OBM must operate in the light—where information is shared. God is love, truth and light. The *master of deceit* hides in darkness because his evil is exposed in light. He deceives executives into believing they should not trust employees with information. This creates problems, rather than solving them.

> *We love customer complaints because we will do our best to set things right.*
>
> **Clark Johnson,
> CEO,
> Pier One Imports**

Life and Death

When God created earth and man, he delegated to man and commanded, *Take on my image — be fruitful and increase, fill and subdue and rule over the earth.* Two things He did not relinquish were control over life and death. Life is not only physical, but mental (the soul) and spiritual. Heaven is for our soul and our spirit.

WHY DO PARTICIPATORY "PROFIT/QUALITY" IMPROVEMENT PROGRAMS WORK?

They treat the individual with respect

They communicate and give feedback

They create a sense of family and recognize team work

They teach about and build character

They demonstrate and teach honesty

They lessen jealousy by the use of numbers for comparisons

WHY DON'T THEY WORK?

Lack of trust of management's intentions by employees

Doubt that the ideas contributed will be used

Jealousy

Bitterness

Resentment

Poor communication (both ways)

HIS PRINCIPLES WORK FOR EVERYONE WHO USES THEM.

Even with the blessings He provides us through our lives by way of His active involvement, one magnificent event brings Him more joy than any other: the creation of new life. God picks the color of eyes, the personality, talents, and physical size — even the purpose for an individual's life. We may perform a sexual act but conception is His choice. Taking a life before birth is an abomination to Him and to all that He has created. Someone would love every child, if it were given the chance to live.

> *Men Who Do Not Know Him But Follow His Truths Will Be Blessed.*

Our will cannot take precedence over His. He gave us dominion over the earth, but life and death are also spiritual and go beyond our responsibilities. Death by the hand of another man, outside of the punishment for violation of laws and certain acts of war, is also an abomination to God. Life is eternal, so His timing, just as in creation, is critical for the spiritual life of each person entering heaven or hell. At the same time, the death of a loved one often has a great impact and spurs character growth in those left behind. God sees the big picture and has the ideal time for each of us to live and die.

Forgiveness
vs. Rejection

Clearing the record of those who have wronged me and bearing no grudge against them.

CHARACTER
TRAINING
INSTITUTE

A Change of Heart

Making a shrewd family and business decision, Terry Jennings, a real estate investor, created a franchise from his parents' moderately successful deli-restaurant. The franchise was in partnership with his sister, who earnestly wanted her own business. The franchise fee would serve as a fine pension for his parents, who would need it in later years.

In the first two years of operation, the restaurant, which opened across town, exceeded projections. Terry's sister managed the restaurant with his part-time assistance. As they planned to open another restaurant, an investigative reporter from a local TV station, trying to gain notoriety, sensationalized some union participation violations noted by the city inspector. Most people agreed the TV story was a set-up, but there was nothing Terry could do.

Business fell off by 50%. Terry was enraged. He vowed revenge, and began developing a plot to catch the reporter in a drug bust on videotape. He hired a private investigator from another station to tail the reporter and learn about his every move. He had decided to videotape his set-up and distribute the tape to government officials and the media all over the city.

In the midst of his planning, a close business associate invited Terry to his house to meet with some men who shared and prayed for each other weekly. Terry was impressed by the commitment of the men. They noted that he was full of hate and asked him to share his frustration. Their advice to him was to think before going ahead with his plan, and to pray about it, telling Terry that if he followed through with his plan, he would become just like the man who had harmed him.

Terry soon realized that his hatred and plan for revenge was only hurting him. He began praying for the reporter, and forgave him. Terry said, *It was like the world's troubles were taken off my shoulders.*

MORAL OF THE STORIES:

1. This Truth and character quality speaks to the heart of *Love your neighbor* and The Golden Rule. Loving (caring, empathy, trust, kindness, openness and a sincere desire to help) the employees, customers, suppliers, vendors, community, and stockholders is what drives the ongoing success of a business. The Lord knew this when He gave Moses The Ten Commandments. It is part of His design, in harmony with the culture, environment and human sensitivities that He built into us.

2. Good communication from the executive level down, as well as back up to top management, is absolutely critical in business. As in a family, a business must communicate internally in an honest and loving way. With poor or little feedback, we "miss the mark" and harm our business potential to be successful, and the relationships that we attempt to establish with all parties.

3. We all make mistakes and "fall short" of the intent of a righteous God. However, He has forgiven us through His son. It is our responsibility to forgive those who have done wrong against us. If we do not, we will suffer the consequences within our spirit of frustration, bitterness, and hate that can lead to stress, then to physical illness, a decline in business success or other problems.

4. Our motive is key. If we want to accomplish something by manipulating people with circumstances or money for our self-centered gain, it runs in conflict with all the principles God has established. We should not be self-centered but God-centered, and servants to our fellowman.

5. Many companies miss reaching their full potential because they focus on the wrong motive of making money, rather than on ways to serve (love) the customers (all parties). Serve first, and the money will follow as a reward, not as a purpose.

6. Downsizing for the personal gain of a few or to benefit stockholders who do not work in the business, is done with the wrong motive. Downsizing, if not handled properly, can break the spirit of a company. It can break the momentum needed in business for achieving admirable goals. Downsizing because of a change in the market, if it is for the good of the majority, the future health of the business, and if it's in the customers' best interest can be the correct decision. How it is handled and how people are treated through the process (ideally, with love, care and fairness) is critical. The same is true for the employee who leaves the company. His resignation should be handled with respect, fairness and kindness.

Why did God let my friend die?

In pain, suffering people ask, *why did God let my friend (wife, child, husband, mother, father) die prematurely?* Jim Brewer says, *for the same reason that he let His son die.* All who die prematurely do so because of missing God's mark, or sin (personal, family, corporate or national). God can empathize with human pain because of the sacrifice He made of His own son, to die a physical death for our mistakes.

Yet to God, death is never final. There is a life beyond this earthly body.

Consider God's perspective. In allowing death, adversity, and sacrifice, God makes it possible for humans to learn about Him and draw closer to His plan. At death, who normally feels the greatest impact? The person who died, or those left behind? How many prayers are said for that person and his or her family? How much repentance occurs? How many lives are changed or redirected because of the loss or sacrifice of another human?

7   Forgiveness is not an option for any of us, it's a necessity. Others will offend or harm us; unfortunately, some of us will do the same to others. We are all at different levels of character growth. Often others don't mean to hurt us, but they reflect the hurt they feel inside and try to give it to us. Our job is to forgive and pray for them; otherwise, the bitterness we allow to live in our heart will harm us more than it harms them.

8. *"Do unto others as you would have them do unto you"* is The Golden Rule.

9. Operate your business in the light, (God is light) not in the darkness. Look at *Open Book Management* and all other programs which communicate trust and raise productivity and human achievement in business.

What Do We Worship?

Anger can be acquired from a parent or through the seed words of bitterness, hate, or jealousy which take root in the spirit, build up and finally are released through yelling or violent acts. Anger is actually a defensive mode in which we fight back out of the fear of being hurt. The deep rooted bitterness or hatred in the heart can only be cured through the healing power of the Word or prayer, which are spiritual. *Psychological counseling might help, but it seldom gets to the root of spiritual damage without the Word of God and prayer.*

Some Practical Ways
Employers Can Love Their Employees

Love is	Filter	To show love, the company can use
Patient	**Are**	Strategic planning process, Listening, Empowering
Not angry		Involvement Lay out time table
Convicting		Accountable
Tough *		Measure TQM
Kind	**Company**	Smile, act caring, concerned Rewards Recognize Terminates with respect, help Involve family or associates
Not boastful		Watches the tongue
Not evil		No false idols
Not rude	**Leaders**	Act and teach respect, management
Truthful		Communicate bad as well as good news
Not self seeking Not proud Not boastful		Humble toward others Recognizes people Gives credit to deserving
Forgiving		Policy - we learn from mistakes, take risks, no reprimands
Protects	**Walking**	Good financing package for stability Defends legally
Trusts		Self-directed work teams Delegates authority Back-up people
Hopes	**The**	Communication Share vision, dreams often Research for future
Preserves	**Talk?**	Profit sharing, ESOP 401K, bonus, new job opportunities, create new companies

* Tough love is added to I Corinthians 13:4

Movement To And From His Truths

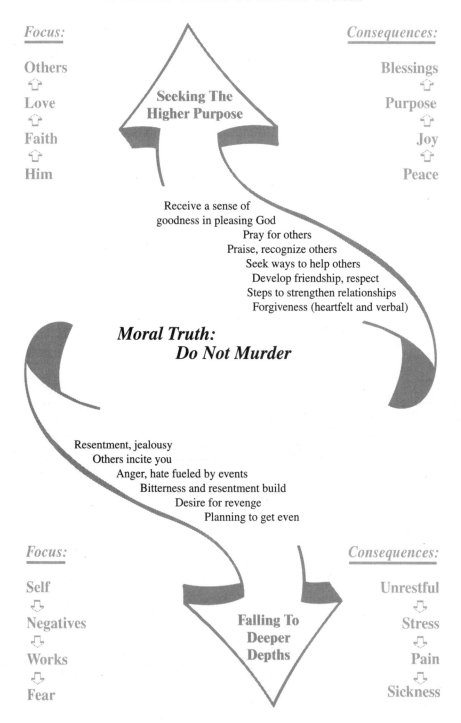

Focus:

Others
⇧
Love
⇧
Faith
⇧
Him

Consequences:

Blessings
⇧
Purpose
⇧
Joy
⇧
Peace

Seeking The Higher Purpose

Receive a sense of
goodness in pleasing God
Pray for others
Praise, recognize others
Seek ways to help others
Develop friendship, respect
Steps to strengthen relationships
Forgiveness (heartfelt and verbal)

Moral Truth:
Do Not Murder

Resentment, jealousy
Others incite you
Anger, hate fueled by events
Bitterness and resentment build
Desire for revenge
Planning to get even

Focus:

Self
⇩
Negatives
⇩
Works
⇩
Fear

Consequences:

Unrestful
⇩
Stress
⇩
Pain
⇩
Sickness

Falling To Deeper Depths

WELL DONE, FAITHFUL SERVANT

Moral Truth: *Do not commit adultery.*

Character Quality: *Be faithful and loyal.*

Evil Turned Good

Lee Ezell was born and raised near Philadelphia by her mother and alcoholic father. At a Billy Graham Crusade, Lee made a commitment to Christ. After graduating from high school she was determined to seek a new life. At 18, she left home and moved to Northern California. After work on the first day in her first job, she was raped by another employee.

That night is horrible in her mind but she dusted herself off and tried to move ahead. In those days, there was no place to turn for rape counseling, and she certainly did not want to go to the police. Instead she bawled her eyes out; she sensed a guilt she could not shake. Months later she went to her doctor because of feeling sick and he told her she was pregnant. She said, *That can't be.* Upset and distraught, she moved to southern California and happened to attend a church where she struck up a friendship with an older couple. The Bible verse, Psalm 139, inspired her to reject abortion. The couple took her into their home until the baby was born. She did not believe that she could raise a young child as a teenager with no husband, so she gave the baby up for adoption the night it was born.

She had a number of up-and-down experiences but ten years later finally married a wonderful man who had two children of his own. She told him about the rape and child and he could relate because of similar losses in his life.

Years later she received a phone call. The voice on the other end said, *Hello, my name is Julie. You've never met me but I'm your daughter and you are a grandmother.* Julie's adopted parents had raised her as a Christian.

To help relieve Lee's anxiety at meeting Julie face-to-face, Lee's husband talked to Julie's husband, telling him that she was conceived in rape. At first it was hard for her to accept but she later would ask her mother, *Have you ever seen this scripture in Psalm 139:13-16 'You knit me together in my mother's womb, all the days ordained for me were written in Your book before one of them came to be.' If this is true then God wanted me to be born.*

Lee became not only a successful wife and mother but also a sought-after public speaker. She said, *God does not cause evil but has a way of taking tragedy and turning it into a blessing. I found my missing piece and I believe others can too.* Both Lee and Julie have written a book, *The Missing Piece,* and have been on national talk shows and shared their message of hope and encouragement with thousands of people.

Caring Makes Sense

At the Hyatt Hotel Corporation, their chairman, Derryl Hartley-Leonard, established a program called FORCE which encourages every manager to take off four paid days a year to volunteer in community activities. Hartley-Leonard estimates that, in a given month, about a thousand Hyatt employees are out in the community getting involved. Each summer Hyatt hires ten interns from local schools and community

CHARACTER QUALITY

- *Be Faithful and Loyal* -

Adultery is not only sexual in nature, but also is defined as the violation of the personal relationship or covenant (emotional or physical) between people or groups. Far too often, violations of relationships occur between employer and employee, customers and others. It is caused by the deceptive image that pleasure or personal gain is more important than principle. It is the false belief that self-discipline, commitment, faithfulness and integrity went out of style in the 1950's. The media image says you have to get all the "gusto" while you can.

Senator Bob Packwood was a great supporter of women's rights and abortion. Yet, at the same time he was an adulterer who violated his relationships with many women and knowingly took advantage of his position. He may be one of the most shameful examples of a public figure who was committed to serve the very group he violated.

Through His truths, God is warning us that wrong acts draw negative consequences — perhaps not today, but eventually. We pay the price here on earth or in the hereafter.

colleges, and more than 300 students from various schools are involved in Hyatt programs.

Many Hyatt Hotels are involved in the Adopt-a-School programs, and Hyatt has pledged more than $250,000 to the American Hotel Foundation (the Scholarship subsidiary of the American Hotel and Motel Association), to benefit students seeking degrees in hotel management. Hyatt has also introduced a minority summer internship program.

Hartley-Leonard has learned as he moved up in the Hyatt Corporation that there is no reason to treat people poorly. He began learning this from the Hyatt manager who first hired him almost 32 years ago. Pat Foley was the general manager of a Hyatt in Southern California; Hartley-Leonard came in, destitute and in need of a job. He went up to the desk clerk and asked if they were taking job applications. Someone made a derogatory remark about his "limey" (Irish) accent, and Foley came out of his office and began to talk with him. *He was of Irish heritage, too, so we joked about that*, remembers Hartley-Leonard. *He asked me what I was doing, and I explained it to him, and, sure enough, he offered me a job.*

Foley then asked Hartley-Leonard how he would get to work; upon hearing that the young man would take the bus, as he had no car, Foley took him by the arm and led him across the street to a bank, where Foley co-signed an $800 car loan. *That was probably one of the most significant things. . . that framed how I approach employees. Foley taught me that when you have power over other people, you give up the right to abuse them.*

Unfaithfulness

In the 1960s America elected a President who had charm, looks, intelligence and confidence. While he was wealthy and thought to come from a good home. He seemed to pick up from his father some bad habits of "womanizing." He told an ambassador in front of others that he had to have sex at least every three days or he would get headaches. He discussed it with some reporters, and propositioned women openly during his travels.

His affair with Marilyn Monroe was well documented, and he finally broke it off after she pestered the White House staff who believed that she thought she had become the "second lady." At that time the media didn't report such stories or scandals because of their commitment to the public and to a nation with moral convictions.

But the Bible says that the sins of the father will affect generations. Certainly the Kennedy family has been greatly affected. There is a price to pay for unfaithfulness. At some point, God will remove His protection over us. Our grace period is over, and we will not be prepared to handle the consequences of our acts.

Employee Loyalty

Compensation Design Group surveyed 500 companies nationwide to determine the loyalty of employees to their employer. Here are the results:

QUESTION	RESPONSE
Loyalty between a company and its employees is said to be disappearing, Do you agree?	• 79% said *yes* and 21% said *no*.
Are you more or less loyal to your company than you were five years ago?	• 29% said *more* and 61% percent said *less*.
Do you feel your company is more loyal or less loyal to you than it was five years ago?	• 22% said *more* and 78% said *less*
Do you plan to remain with your company?	These agreed they would; • 20% of the hourly employees • 5% of clerical • 30% of professional • 35% of middle managers • 50% of executives

Businesses teach values by the commitments they keep or break. How those who are laid off or downsized are treated has a direct bearing on the image, reputation, and integrity of the company, and sends a message louder than their rhetoric.

Employee Thanks

In the 1980s, during the ups and downs of severe competition and recessions, Delta Airlines "bucked the trend" toward laying off employees, valuing employee loyalty and high morale over short-term profits. To show their appreciation

The bridge you burn now may be the one you later have to cross.

and loyalty, Delta employees on their own created a payroll-deduction program for employees to voluntarily contribute to the purchase of a multi-million-dollar airplane for the company.

Most people agree that it's important for good managers to praise and thank employees, but seldom do employees reach out and give positive feedback to their bosses. Executives need love and appreciation just as often as anyone else.

Loyalty

vs. Unfaithfulness

Using difficult times
to demonstrate my commitment
to those whom I have relationships with.

**CHARACTER
TRAINING
INSTITUTE**

Sacrificing For the Few

World Life (fictitious name) was founded 60 years ago in one of our nation's insurance centers in the Midwest. The founder had made great sacrifices in developing and growing the business with a unique niche. His sons grew up in the business. They brought more education and innovation to the company, increasing the customer base throughout 25 states. As is typical in family run business, the third generation, which had not made the same sacrifices, did not have the same appreciation for what their fathers had built.

By the 50th year and beyond, growth became slow, even flat. Rather than replace themselves with more capable management, the owners operated in "their way." While their fathers had contributed greatly to the community and vice versa, they were more complacent about this responsibility.

Finally, the board said "Let's get our stock growing or cash out." Two years later they decided to sell the company because the profits weren't pushing up the stock value. They entertained three bids and finally accepted the highest bid. The buyer let go all the 1,000 employees and just folded World Life customers into their own home operation center in another city.

The community was outraged because of its effort to try to help the company. The employees were bitter, as many had been employed 20-30 years and felt they weren't treated fairly. The two other bidders offered to keep the office open and keep the majority of employees, but the officers took the less courageous way out, using the excuse that they were afraid some stockholder might sue them for accepting a lesser bid.

Rather than sharing some of the economic benefits with loyal employees and community, they chose to maximize their own personal returns.

The Loyalty Effect

Frederick Reichheld, director of Bain & Company, a leading strategic consulting firm and author of *The Loyalty Effect*, has studied and researched economic and social effects of employee and customer retention for a number of years. His theme is that a company's focus should not be on short-term profits but on *value creation*, an attitude and philosophy about how to run a business.

In an era when companies typically lose half their employees every four years, half their customers in five years, and half their investors within a year, Reichheld uses as an illustration that a credit card company which retains just 5% of its customers each year will see profits rise 75% from that customer. He uses examples from a number of companies which began with some form of the Golden Rule.

In the restaurant industry, store manager turnover is 30-40% a year, but Chick-Fil-A loses only 4-6%. It is not untypical for restaurants to have a 300% turnover in hourly crew each year, but Chick-Fil-A averages 120%. One reason? After two years of employment, young employees can receive scholarship money toward college tuition.

In another example, Pizza Hut store mangers can earn an additional $1,500 for exceeding their profit projections by $10,000. Chick-Fil-A store operators share in 50% of profits. Dan Cathy says of Chick-Fil-A's success, *It's not the recipe for the sandwich, or the food quality, or the mall concept, or the training. These are all important, but the key is our operators— their capabilities and our relationships with them. Over time, our system will change and evolve so that it can use the full potential of our best operators.*

Morally Right versus Morally Wrong

Louisiana Pacific and Masonite are both manufacturers of pressed board siding for homes. Both companies have run into difficulty in terms of the life expectancy of the product. This has resulted in settlements with property owners, either individually or through a series of class action suits. Whether for the right reasons or not, they made the right moral decision, to compensate customers for buying a poor-quality product.

On the other hand, the Manville Corporation which manufactured asbestos, ran into difficulties in the 1970s and 1980s through the discovery of poisoning of children exposed to asbestos in ceiling tiles in schools and other institutions. Rather than try to do right by its customers, it chose to do right by its stockholders. It filed for re-organization under Chapter Eleven bankruptcy laws. Federal Judge James H. Sarokin of Newark, New Jersey said that Manville *manipulated the judicial system so as to delay thousands of claimants and denied completely to some their day in court to present asbestos related injuries.*

In 1982 the "Tylenol scare" cost Johnson & Johnson $250 million when they yanked their products off shelves throughout the country. Their action was voluntary and swift. Their CEO claimed the reason for their decision was self-evident. They referred to their corporate credo and philosophy of serving their customers first in making their decision. The

A Great Place To Work

Robert Levering wrote the book, *A Great Place to Work*, after researching hundreds of companies and asking employees what they expected out of a great place to work. Here are the five common threads that most often were mentioned:

1. A friendly place to work.
2. Very little politics in the office.
3. Getting a fair shake from your employer.
4. An opportunity that is more than a job.
5. It seems just like a family.

Here are the words used most often by the employees:

1. Trust.
2. Pride in their organization.
3. Freedom.
4. Fair treatment.
5. Mistakes are allowed.

correct moral and ethical decision by Johnson & Johnson has won national acclaim, as Tylenol sales continue to grow each year.

The companies who choose the "short term win/lose" approach over what is morally right long term in serving their customers, commit a type of adultery. These are the types of organizations and individuals which energize our legislators to write and pass more legislation enforcing the truths which are the foundation for our business ethics.

Finding an Answer

Charles Duke walked on the moon but his wife, Dotty, was in depression. She wanted love from Charlie and sought real fulfillment. After the space program, Charlie and a partner started their own business with the goal of making money.

He was a workaholic and didn't provide the love Dotty wanted. She searched, reasoned, and struggled; she tried drugs to the point of near-suicide. She saw no hope, even though they went to church every week. She had studied religions in college and was taught that they were all the same, that the key was just to love one another. So she didn't know if God existed.

Charlie and Dotty went to a church meeting where a speaker shared why Jesus was different, and that He answered prayer. Dotty decided that she would make a commitment to "try" Jesus. Christ then answered so many of her prayers she knew He was real.

But she struggled with forgiving Charlie for the things he had done to offend her. She had been putting her husband before God, and started to realize that only God could provide the love that she needed in order to be fulfilled. She realized her husband was not God.

Charlie was unfulfilled in his business. Two-and-a-half years later, through a Bible study he made his own commitment to the Lord. Their marriage was energized. Charlie said, *It costs the government millions for me to walk on the moon for three days, and my walk with the Lord is free and will last a lifetime and beyond.*

This is the 1990s

Recently, Disney, American Express and IBM have pioneered the concept of providing health insurance benefits to partners of homosexual employees. Their commitment was obviously based on two factors: economic and humanitarian. The new insurance benefit offers gay employees an incentive to stay with their companies. As well, in an effort to do "what is right" they believe each person has rights and should be treated fairly. On the surface, it appears to fit with God's moral laws of *loving your neighbor as yourself*.

God appreciates that attitude and loves the homosexual as much as he loves anyone. However, homosexuality is about fornication and living in deceit. Same sex partners don't reproduce or make a family unit by God's standard. Homosexuality is an emotional and spiritual problem psychologists can't correct. Only through God's grace can it be healed and there are many examples of it being done every day.

With a media attitude that adultery or fornication have no relevance because *this is the 90s* , many major corporations are "too smart" and too much in-control of themselves to turn to a loving God for His involvement in helping them and their employees. However, the real solution is spiritual counseling for these employees.

There is always a long-term consequence for *missing the mark* of His truths. Even if the consequences are not immediately seen in economic problems, there is still a great potential of creating internal morale problems of jealousy.

Truth For Both Good and Evil

How can a loving God allow people to be financially successful by selling pornography or drugs?

> *Decisions can take you out of God's will but never out of His reach.*

1. His truths work for all of us. The pornography or drug dealers are showing a love for the customer, filling their needs. Unfortunately, they are emotionally sick people, worshipping false idols of lust or addiction, leading to more sin. The business then takes advantage of the customer's weakness.

2. God does not see the financial return as Godly success—only as a measure of exchange. Our world wrongfully looks at wealth as the main indicator of success.

3. God wants to heal these people, as He wants to heal everyone. He does not look at the pornography or drug dealer as worse sinners than those who lie to their boss or spouse or steal from the office. He wants all of us to repent, give up our ways and come to Him.

4. If the pornography or drug dealers do not repent or receive punishment from the local authorities, then they will face the vengeance of God on earth or in the next life.

Foregoing Profits

Jack Eckerd, founder of the multibillion dollar drugstore chain, received a letter in 1971 from a customer. She said, *You should be ashamed of some of the filth you sell in your stores.* As a result of this letter, Jack urged his Board and got their commitment to drop the pornography literature that they sold in 1,700 stores. Initially they lost several million dollars in sales as a result of that action, but they also got thousands of letters of support, and sales rebounded.

> *Kindness is the oil that takes the friction out of life.*

Deeply touched, Jack wrote to the president of other drug chains and urged them to do the same. As a result, seven drug chains and one national convenience store chain did the same thing.

Years later Jack became a spiritual Christian at the age of 70. He always considered himself a good man and attended church regularly, but his new commitment changed his life as well as his motives. People said he was more at peace with himself and showed a *greater love in his heart*.

The National Coalition Against Pornography would like for Congress to pass a law prohibiting businesses from selling pornography. Whether this happens or not, there is a higher law of morality calling us to do the right thing—not just for ourselves, but for our children, and because of the pain inflicted through the perpetuation of sexual lust. At the same time, this story is a heart warming example of how a CEO's moral decisions can influence so many lives.

THE MORAL OF THE STORIES:

1. Our relationships with other people are not to be forsaken when they become difficult or frustrating. Life's relationships are about win-win, not win-lose. *What goes around, comes around,* but what is most important is mutual respect and a love-based attitude

that serves the will of our Creator, placing our fellowman's interests over our self-centered needs. Business and life are team sports and the best players are willing to sacrifice themselves for the team.

2. We each need to look seriously at our personal and corporate decisions with a vision to the future. Will our decision adversely affect the health of the business and the relationship we have with all our customer groups? How would we like to be treated? The short term and least expensive way is not always a long-term win-win.

3. Are we loyal to our existing customers or always chasing new ones at a higher cost, to make a better deal? Peter Drucker says, *a business has a 1 in 16 chance of doing business with a new customer, a 1 in 4 chance of doing business with a former customer, and a 1 in 2 chance of doing more business with an existing customer.*

4. Are we spending enough time with our spouse and loved ones, instead of adulterating our relationship because of our own personal wants, habits or the chasing of "success"?

5. Treat fairly the employees we have to let go and give them a good chance to find a new job.

6. When you resign, do it with integrity, appreciation and good will. Be a good example to others. Living by the Golden Rule is good personal and corporate policy.

7. Treat those in relationship with you better than their expectations and you will be an example that others will emulate.

What Do We Worship?

Lust is an unreasonable desire, most commonly for power, possessions, or sexual release. Sexual desire for a man is a craving and crying out for love. Men, more than women, express love through the sexual act. Sexual lust is a way to fill a spiritual void and hurt. It becomes a passion through mental pictures; that is how pornography, suggestive TV, commercials and clubs perpetuate the problem and stir up cravings.

Movement To And From His Truths

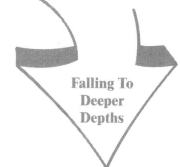

Focus:

Others
⇧
Love
⇧
Faith
⇧
Him

**Seeking The
Higher Purpose**

Consequences:

Blessings
⇧
Purpose
⇧
Joy
⇧
Peace

Become more loyal, supportive
Take initiative to help
Offer to help others
Pray for others
Open heart, inner cleansing
Seek ways to change
Seek forgiveness
Self realization of faults

Moral Truth:
Do Not Commit Adultery

Eyes on appeal of others
Inner hurt, self-pity
Desire to be more happy
Believe "new" relationshipis answer
Secret acts that break relationships
Lying, denial
Broken relationships

Focus:

Self
⇩
Negatives
⇩
Works
⇩
Fear

**Falling To
Deeper
Depths**

Consequences:

Unrestful
⇩
Stress
⇩
Pain
⇩
Sickness

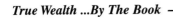

GIVING TOUCHES BOTH HEARTS

Moral Truth: *Do not steal.*

Character Quality: *But give to others.*

To Whom Much is Given

John D. Rockefeller, Sr. drove himself hard to be successful in business. At the age of 33, he had made his first million dollars. By dedicating every waking moment to his work, at 43, he controlled the biggest business in the world. By the age of 53, he had become the richest man on earth, the world's only billionaire at that time.

For his achievements, however, he bartered his own happiness and health. He developed alopecia, a condition in which not only the hair on the head drops out but also most of the hair from the eyelashes and eyebrows. One biographer said he looked like a mummy. His weekly income was a million dollars, but his digestion was so bad he could eat only crackers and milk.

Newspapers pictured him as an industrial pirate and men that worked for him in the oil fields hung him in effigy. Body guards watched him day and night. He found little peace or happiness in the wealth that he had accumulated. He couldn't sleep well and enjoyed very few things.

At 53 he was a frail man and newspaper writers had already written his obituary. One night when he couldn't sleep, he came to a spiritual realization that his wealth would do him no good in his life beyond—that money must not be hoarded but shared for the benefit of others. The next morning he got up and established the Rockefeller Foundation, which probably has had its greatest philanthropic impact on medicine, eliminating hookworm, providing penicillin, and saving millions from death by malaria, tuberculosis, diphtheria and many other diseases.

No one expected John D. Rockefeller to live past his 53rd birthday but after that night his health started to improve dramatically. Rockefeller was a Christian, and a giver who recognized that he had a God-given talent for making money. He died at age 98 with the understanding, *To whom much is given, much is required.*

Milking Us

Stew Leonard's dairy store in Norwalk, Connecticut was considered to be one of the great entrepreneurial successes and role models for American business in the mid 1980s. The family store was a unique shopping experience with fresh produce, meats, dairy products (plus animated animals and things for kids). It was larger than the typical supermarket with three times the volume. People traveled for miles because of the quality of the products and the experience of shopping in his store. Tom Peters and others shared Stew's great success with business executives around the country. Even major corporations wanted to learn how and what principles were used to accomplish so much.

However, on a trip to St. Martin in the Caribbean, Stew and his family had some difficulty getting through customs with $75,000 in cash. There is a limit on how much cash the US government will allow you to take out of the country at any one time. Because of this incident, federal agents started doing some investigations and discovered that he had diverted

CHARACTER QUALITY

- *Give To Others* -

Stealing money and possessions are self-centered acts. Surveys conclude that it costs the average American $200 a year in increased prices to cover the economic losses businesses suffer from retail theft alone.

However, many Americans have a giving heart and understand the principle of *give and it will be given unto you.* In 1995, the American Association of Fund Raisers estimated that Americans give $144 billion a year to various charities, of which 45% goes to religious organizations. Additional non-monetary giving represents billions more in time, compassion and caring that comes from the heart. This contrasts to the situation in countries where the government supports churches or charities with tax money; there, resentment is created.

The message comes through over and over again, do not be self-centered but be centered toward giving and helping others. As we give, our hearts are touched, and we benefit. The receiver's heart is warmed, and a natural desire to give back continues the cycle. As we give the customer what he wants, he gives us his loyalty with the potential to become a customer for life. Give first with no expected return—don't wait for others to give to you.

more than $17 million from income tax. Leonard was ordered to repay the stolen tax money and fined $850,000. At 63 years of age he was sentenced to 52 months in federal prison. Hoarding wealth beyond our reasonable and future needs works against God's plan for your life and those you could touch. When God's truths are violated, negative consequences will eventually occur.

One Billion Dollars

> *You can't take your money with you, but you can send it on ahead.*

Ted Turner in his pledge to give a billion dollars to the United Nations, said, *I'm not really giving away that much, It's only a third of my net worth, money I didn't know what to do with anyway.* Jesus said, *'The real givers are like the lady who had nothing but gave away the two coins, all she had to live on.'* Also the washerwoman from Mississippi who recently gave her $150,000 life savings away, are the real examples for us, not me.

Dying Rich

John D. Rockefeller had an influence on many men, one of whom was Andrew Carnegie, one of America's true industrial giants at the turn of the century. In 1889 Andrew Carnegie wrote an article in the North American Review in which he said, *The man who dies rich, dies disgraced. . . The day is not far distant when the man who dies leaving behind millions of available wealth which was free for him to administer during life will pass away unwept, unhonored and unsung.*

> *Money is not a measure of blessing, but of responsibility.*

Rockefeller wrote to Carnegie after reading the article, *I wish that more men of wealth were doing as you are doing with your money, but be assured that your example will bear fruit.*

The Calling Card

While he was in the Air Force, Aunt Della sent Wally Amos shoe boxes full of her delicious cookies. If there was anyone well-liked on the US military base in Korea, it was Wally Amos. When he returned home he went through a period of frustration in finding the right job. As he made sales calls he would take some of the cookies that he learned to make from

Aunt Della, as his calling card. People loved them and urged him to start his own cookie company.

But Wally had more important things to do—his goal was to make it big time in the entertainment industry. His marriage suffered and after thirteen years it ended in divorce. One day he pulled together his three sons in his 1960 Rambler and headed to the Grand Canyon. Little did he know that there, the beauty and splendor of God's work would draw him spiritually back to the roots and heritage he had known as a young man in church.

> *A hundred times a day I remind myself that my life depends on the labors of other men, living and dead, and that I must exert myself to give in the measure as I have received.*
>
> **Albert Einstein**

As he returned home, a new man with a new vision, he realized that his gift was in giving away cookies and pleasing people. This Godly inspiration led him to Famous Amos Cookie Shops, and later a world-wide distribution company.

Generosity
VS. STINGINESS

Realizing that I am only a steward of all I have and using it for His best purposes.

CHARACTER TRAINING INSTITUTE

The Marketing Strategy With A Heart

Without fully understanding the *invisible economy*, individuals and companies are using the giving principle and receiving multiple returns. Giving to the United Way, to churches, to golf tournament charities, and to homeless people are just some of the thousands of ways that we change the lives of others. But the motive needs to be unselfish, if blessings are to follow.

The key is the relationship of trust and love generated by giving first with no expected return. We have all seen men and women executives of companies giving their time and money to important causes. There is a loving God rewarding that type of unselfish behavior in ways we don't even fathom.

Giving for the Right Reason

In 1987, Jack Eckerd sold the most profitable drug store chain in the United States. He credits his father's teaching of honesty, hard work and determination as his way of dealing with people. He said, *I made up my mind I would never do anything, if I could help it, that wasn't in the best interest of the customers, the employees and the stockholders.*

Jack was always a very giving man. He started a youth camp for troubled youth, that now operates in several states, and devoted a lot personal time to the creation and operation of PRIDE for prison inmates, to teach work ethics and skills that can better prepare them to return to society, more productive.

Yet, at 70, he turned his life over to the leading of the Lord. He found a deeper and more meaning in his walk. *I discovered my thinking was all wrong. I had been number one and everything revolved around me. God has an awful lot of patience. His unmerited favor was working in me and through me.*

Something his father told him really began to ring true. *You'll enjoy giving money a lot more if you do it quietly, because then you don't have to wonder if you gave because you wanted recognition or because you were helping people.*

Servant Leadership

Bill Pollard, of ServiceMaster, the multi-billion dollar public company, in his book, *The Soul of the Firm*, relates these comments: *Socrates said that a person should first understand oneself as a means of making contributions to others. 'Know thyself' was his advice.' Aristotle counseled his followers that to 'use one's talents to the utmost, one must have discretion and direction.' His advice was to 'control thyself.' But another great thinker changed history — and the hearts of people — with his unique approach to a meaningful life. 'Give thyself' were the spoken words of Jesus. In John 13 we read the story of how Jesus took a towel and a basin of water and washed the disciples' feet. In doing so, He taught his disciples that no leader is greater than the people he leads, and that even the humblest of tasks is worthy for a leader to do.*

Does this example fit in today's world, 2000 years later? There certainly is no scarcity of feet to wash, and towels are always available. I suggest that the only limitation, if there is one, involves the ability of each of us as leaders to get on our hands and knees, to compromise our pride, to be involved, and to have compassion for those we serve.

Bill continues, *For people to grow and develop within the firm, its leaders and managers must be prepared to serve as part of their leadership. Servant leadership is part of our ethic, and it means that leaders of our firm should never ask anyone to do anything they are not willing to do themselves. The leader exists, for the benefit of the firm, not the firm for the benefit of the leader. When we lead by serving, we are committed to be an example for others to follow, initiator for change and growth, and an activist for the future.*

Giving Back

Having been left with his brother in an orphanage to be raised, Pat Kelly, now CEO of Physician Sales & Service (PSS), felt God had done him wrong by not giving him the opportunity to have a normal family life with a mother and father. After the age of 6, he only saw his father twice before he died. But Pat learned a lesson in the orphanage he may have never learned if he'd had a normal family upbringing. He learned to share and get along with 60 other kids. This is a principle that dramatically influenced his entire leadership style,

> *We make a living by what we get...*
> *We make a life by what we give.*

119

and helped to foster his company's innovation using Open Book Management concepts.

Having recently had the opportunity to visit another much larger orphanage, Boys Town in Nebraska, Pat was deeply touched. His personal mission in life has changed because of this experience. His new goal is to give $100 million to the Virginia Home For Boys where he was raised.

Pat is just an example of many successful Americans who offer scholarships. Organizations like the Rotary, Kiwanis Foundations, Gold Tournament, and the Horatio Alger Association help needy young people, giving them scholarships and opportunities they could have never dreamed about otherwise.

Never Stop Giving

Larry Dobbs, a salesman for the Lakeland Ledger, loved cars so much that in 1978, he quit his job "cold turkey" to start a new business publishing a newsletter for Mustang enthusiasts. However, Larry and his wife had a unique perspective: they decided to tithe 10 percent to the Lord from day one.

In twenty years of business and eight automobile magazines, God provided in every crisis. When he told his advisory group his enthusiasm for the business was gone, they urged him to sell the business. He sold the business a year later for six times the appraised value. In keeping with his faith, he tithed 10 percent as well as gave $1.8 million to his approximately 75 employees.

A Higher Calling

Reporters and writers are still asking Bill McCartney why he gave up a very successful college football career to begin a movement known as *Promise Keepers* which shares the gospel with men in major stadiums across the country. In

Those who bring sunshine to the lives of others cannot keep it from themselves.

just six years the meetings have gone from a handful of men to well over a million attending their weekend conferences. Their ministry continues to explode and gross income alone this year will be over $140 million.

Reporters say, *You must have had a great marketing strategy. Who did you learn from? How did you see or predict this would happen?* Repeatedly McCartney says, *This is not me. It is not one man. It is not a group of men. It is a movement of the Spirit of God. I am merely giving my will to His calling with hundreds of men and organizers because it is so fulfilling to us and pleasing to Him. As we give to Him, he gives back to us with a sense of deep love, joy and commitment to purpose.*

THE MORAL OF THE STORIES:

1. One of our highest callings is in giving and not taking. God pours out abundant blessings on those who give first, with the motive of loving one another. Those with a Godly motive can see depth in the phrase, *It is in giving that we receive.*

2. To rob, steal, or take from another individual is selfishness. Some might feel they gain a temporary advantage in a short-term way. But ultimately it comes back to harm the inner being and spirit through a sense of guilt, uneasiness, anxiety or hatred.

3. Even if we are not reprimanded, accused or convicted over an unlawful act, we lose anyway. If we don't suffer the consequences or seek forgiveness here on earth, we will have to deal with the consequences in the next life.

4. Personal volunteering and heartfelt giving is about *sowing and reaping.* We are affected these ways by volunteering and giving:
   — Fosters relationships between people.
   — Touches the heart of the giver.
   — Touches the heart of the receiver.
   — The receiver senses more responsibility to use the gift wisely.
   — The receiver senses a desire to give back.
   — The cycle grows and more hearts are touched.
   — People grow.
   — God is working in each heart.

5. When the giving is *impersonal* (through taxation and given by a government for welfare, foreign aid, education, etc.), it becomes entitlement. Eventually this aid is resented, as *'not enough,'* because dependancy has been created and human initiative dampened. Impersonal giving dilutes the impact of God's truth working on individual lives. The potential for blessings are limited, and the growth cycles reduced.

6. The *Wall Street Journal* recently reported on the pirating of American videos and CDs.The losses to firms are estimated at $3.5 billion from Chinese and four other nations. Because of recent U.S. trade negotiations, the Chinese have agreed to crack down on the offenders. *It is the Lord's challenge to America to teach the moral truths (His ethics) to the rest of the world.*

7. *Love your neighbor as yourself* (but not their money or possessions).

What Do We Worship?

Greed—Money is important and necessary, but it is the love of money which hurts the human spirit. Having money becomes a craving or passion that becomes a measure of self-worth for many individuals. Without money, they consider themselves failures, and they measure the worth of others by it. This attitude creates an imbalance in a person's life because worshipping their idol, money, can destroy a marriage, family, friendship, or a business. God gives some people talent to create capital and wealth, just as he gives an athlete great ability, but if they live their life for this one master it can destroy them in the long run.

Many executives who were deprived in their youth have taken on the god of money as a way to overcome the hurt that remains in the *underdog mentality*, while others catch the sickness from their parents' attitudes. God wants many of us to be successful financially, but He also wants us to give back generously, not to look at money as a god. Unless you want to be buried in your Cadillac, money will do you no good after your death. Money cannot buy anything eternal.

Movement To And From His Truths

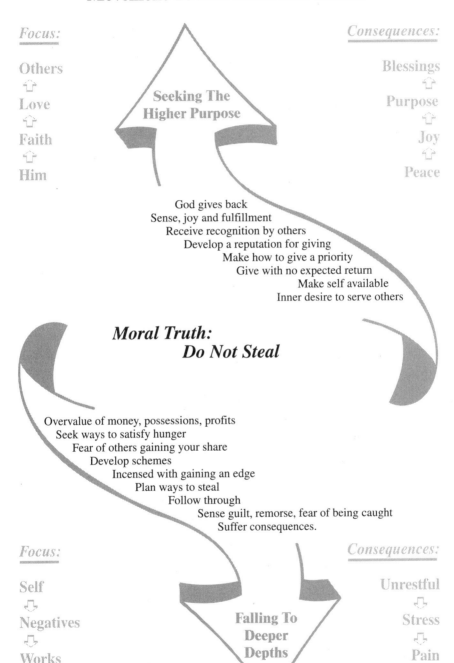

Focus:

Others
⇧
Love
⇧
Faith
⇧
Him

**Seeking The
Higher Purpose**

Consequences:

Blessings
⇧
Purpose
⇧
Joy
⇧
Peace

God gives back
Sense, joy and fulfillment
Receive recognition by others
Develop a reputation for giving
Make how to give a priority
Give with no expected return
Make self available
Inner desire to serve others

Moral Truth:
Do Not Steal

Overvalue of money, possessions, profits
Seek ways to satisfy hunger
Fear of others gaining your share
Develop schemes
Incensed with gaining an edge
Plan ways to steal
Follow through
Sense guilt, remorse, fear of being caught
Suffer consequences.

Focus:

Self
⬇
Negatives
⬇
Works
⬇
Fear

**Falling To
Deeper
Depths**

Consequences:

Unrestful
⬇
Stress
⬇
Pain
⬇
Sickness

123

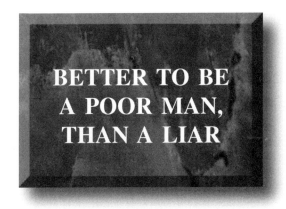

BETTER TO BE A POOR MAN, THAN A LIAR

Moral Truth: *Do not bear false witness.*

Character Quality: *Earn respect through integrity.*

The Used Car Salesman

There is something unusual about Dave Schwartz from Los Angeles. He has sold used cars most of his life, but his philosophy seems to be different. *If something was wrong with a car I was selling, I would rather fix it, and if I couldn't fix it I would tell the prospect up front. If a battery was weak he would know it. If the car used a lot of oil he wouldn't have to drive 100 miles to find out."*

People would tell me, 'Dave, you're nuts. Everybody knows you can't make money in the used car business that way.' For years Dave proved them wrong and succeeded by his methods. One day, a young lady wanted to buy a used car because she had a short assignment in L.A. and wanted something cheap that would just last for the time she was there. After they discussed it, he decided to rent her the car, saving her money and allowing him to make more money, as he could still sell the car or rent it again. This fit with Dave's concern about doing what is right. This way, she would only have the car a short time and have less chance of it having problems.

He discovered a new business concept which became so successful that others wanted to franchise the concept. Today there are several hundred "Rent-a-Wreck" agencies in the United States and Australia. Here is what Dave tells a prospective franchisee. *If money is your only goal, then forget it. I believe that in any enterprise, if you make money your god, then the business will never be really successful. For then you are never satisfied; you've put the cart before the horse.*

He continues, *But if a person enjoys filling needs and making people happy, then there is no end to his success and he doesn't have to worry about money.* It was all put into one sentence two thousand years ago by Jesus Christ when he said: *Whatsoever you would have others do unto you, do unto them.* (Matthew 7:12).

> **The most valuable gift you can give another is a good example.**

Impure Juice

Beech-Nut lost $5 million on sales of $62 million in 1981, and management was under pressure to turn the business around. Buying more expensive apple juice would have worsened the deficit because apple juice was a component in 30% of Beech-Nut sales.

Top executives in the firm decided to make a strategic decision that would be *penny-wise and pound-foolish.* In November, 1987, Beech-Nut Nutrition Corporation, the second largest producer of baby food, pled guilty to 215 felony counts for selling adulterated "bogus" apple food products from 1981 to 1983. Managers thought they were acting shrewdly but the costs to the company and to the owners proved to be anything but shrewd.

CHARACTER QUALITY

- *Earn Respect Through Integrity* -

Abe Lincoln was Postmaster in New Salem, Illinois, from 1833 until the position was abolished. Years later when Lincoln was a struggling attorney, a government official visited his Springfield office, asking for the receipts of $18 which the government had never bothered to collect from the day the Post Office was closed. Lincoln asked the man to wait in his office while he went to his boardinghouse room and brought back a blue sock with silver and copper coins and receipts (the exact sum in coins) and poured it out on the table for the government official. This is an example of Honest Abe *Lincoln's well-known integrity.*

Nothing destroys credibility, creates doubt or puts people on guard faster than realizing or suspecting that someone has lied to them.

The tone and culture established by management has to carry the message to their employees, customers and shareholders about what is right and wrong, or the business's success can be threatened everyday.

Our Creator did not design the body, soul and spirit to carry lies, bitterness or arrogance. If an individual has any grounding in His truth, the spiritual guilt or mental anguish resulting from dishonesty will lead to sickness, frustration or fear. If these negative emotions are held long enough, the body's systems will begin to break down. *Coming clean,* and giving and receiving forgiveness are critical to restore health.

A National Disgrace

Mark Twain is credited with saying *If you tell the truth, you don't have to remember anything.* It is too bad that Richard Nixon did not know Mark Twain. He might have saved all of us from the national disgrace of Watergate. Power, fame, money and success have a tendency to breed egotism in many people. With egotism, people lose sight of reality and take on an "invincible" attitude. Seemingly, they can get along successfully with a few white lies—until the big one comes along that trips them flat on their face.

If Richard Nixon had been humble enough to admit to the American people that he and his people had made a significant mistake, and had apologized in an up front and timely manner, the whole incident would have blown over within two or three months. Everyone would have gotten back to business. Richard Nixon might have been considered one of the best Presidents in our history.

Egotism Causes Forgetfulness

John Wilson, a highly recognized CEO in the Midwest, achieved national notoriety a few years ago. He was interviewed by a well known business newspaper and asked to reveal the secrets of his successful marketing strategy. Flattered, he laid out his strategy and described how he created the system and implemented it.

As the article appeared, a friend of Bill Aronson, a top marketing consultant called him and said, *Isn't that your material that appeared in the business newspaper?* It happened that Bill had shared his concept and strategy three years earlier at an association meeting that John had attended. Unfortunately John forgot where the information had come from; he took it as his own creation, although all materials were copyrighted. No credit was given to Bill and his organization. The issue was settled out of court but it cost John significant money for his *learning curve* experience.

> *The level of motivation in an organization can never rise above the level of trust.*
>
> **Clark Johnson**

128

We All Pay

Price fixing, check fraud schemes, falsifying information for government contracts, savings and loan schemes, insider trading—these are just examples of things that cost businesses and customers billions of dollars each year. The message concerning honesty starts at the top—in the board rooms, in company policies and in business ethics principles that are shared or not shared with employees. The legal costs to prosecute the criminals responsible is staggering; it is a waste of money and an abomination to our Creator's truths and warnings.

Lying For Employment

Bennett Brown, CEO of Enterprise Bank, a healthy young entrepreneurial bank growing at a rapid pace, shares an incident which happened a few years ago when he needed a vice-president for a newly created department. He interviewed an outstanding candidate with significant bank experience. Rather than move quickly in the hiring process as he usually

Loving Employees Serve Better

The American Society for Quality Control reports a study of why customers are lost. Here are their findings:

Perceived indifference by employees 68%

Product dissatisfaction 14%

Competition 9%

Influenced by friends 5%

Move 3%

Death 1%

Total 100%

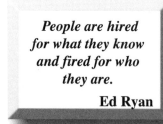

> *People are hired for what they know and fired for who they are.*
>
> **Ed Ryan**

did, he decided to use an outside testing and screening company to help him in his decision. They discovered some discrepancies in the candidate's background and when they confronted him, he admitted that he had "decked" the CEO of the last bank that he had worked for because of his anger with him. This is the reason that he left his last employer off his resume. Don Walker, former FBI agent, reports that it is estimated that 35% of all candidates falsify information about their college on their resumes. This points out that business needs to do its part in exemplifying and teaching the importance of honesty to its people. Otherwise executives are part of the problem and not the solution.

Catch Me, If You Can

The story of Frank Abagnale is true. He ran away from home at age 16 over a broken heart; his parents had announced their divorce. Frank looked older than he actually was and impersonated a pilot for two years, passing bad checks as he went from airline to airline office. Next he impersonated a medical doctor in Atlanta for over a year. In Baton Rouge he passed the bar exam (on the third try), became a lawyer and was the Assistant Attorney General for nearly a year and a half.

He moved to Brigham Young University to impersonate a professor; he had a series of other escapades until he was finally caught in France at the age of 21. By that time, he had passed over $2.5 million in bad checks and was wanted in 13 countries.

He spent time in four different prisons until years later the FBI came to him with an offer to write procedures and policies for securing business systems from white collar crime in exchange for a commuted sentence. A free man, he began a normal life with a family and his own business, helping companies and corporations deal with all of these issues. He stresses to every audience he touches that he made mistakes that he truly regrets. When he left home he gave up any chance of having a half-way normal life and he would love to relive his teenage years.

Big Shots Are In Town

Jon Ledecky, CEO and founder of US Office Products, a $3 billion consolidated company, shares a personal story to make an important point.

Years ago I was a first-year associate in a venture capital firm, and walked in to do due diligence on a business. As my bosses were walking ahead of me, I dropped back and noticed a woman was working furiously assembling some parts. The sweat was coming down her brow. I felt so sorry for her. She reminded me of my mom. With empathy just oozing from my pores, I stepped up and asked, 'How are you doing today?' She said, 'I'm doing fine.' I asked, 'What is it that you're doing?' She saw that all the older guys (because I was about twenty-five at the time) were down the hall. She looked that way, and she looked the other way, and she said, 'Honey, hell if I know. Hired me for the day, said to look busy, some big shots are coming to town.'

> *There's a world of difference between truth and facts. Facts can obscure the truth.*
>
> **Maya Angelou**

Turns out there was no business there. They were scamming the venture capitalists for money. Unfortunately the man ended up in jail, because not only did he have no business, but he also did another incredible trick. He had Price Waterhouse as his accountant. He found the same type font as Price Waterhouse, took the bad report that he was given, retyped it and changed the numbers. he ended up serving about five years in the federal penitentiary. But that happens with dishonest people. You have to be very careful.

Truthfulness vs. deception

Earning Future Trust

By Accurately Reporting Past Facts

CHARACTER
TRAINING
INSTITUTE

Taking a Stand

Larry Rosen has been a highly successful furniture retailer who was convicted by God to develop a code of morals and ethics for his people. He became increasingly concerned about selling his company's largest line of furniture. Larry shared, *We were telling the customers what the manufacturer told us to say, that they are the best in the industry. I knew it wasn't true and it bothered me more and more until finally one day in prayer the Lord worked on my heart. I knew it was time to give up that line of furniture.* Once he did, his sales dropped by 75%, but Larry's conscience was clean. He was at peace over his decision and ready to move on to successfully rebuild his business.

Carl Terzian heads up the largest independent public relations firm in Los Angeles and has many well known clients. What's different about Carl is that in his nearly forty years of business he has never asked a client for a signed contract. Everything is done on a handshake. Clients can leave whenever they like. But this allows him to do the same—to ask a client to leave when he feels his ethics or business practices are not fair or honest.

Some executives say to me, 'But, Carl, you know business is business,' and I say to them, 'That's only a cop-out. You can't forget your fellowman or His values that we all need to live by. Carl says that, *The more companies fail to teach their employees and hold them*

> *To educate a person in the mind and not in morals is to educate a menace to society.*
>
> **Theodore Roosevelt**

accountable to what is right and wrong, the more our nation will have to pass laws to try to legislate the individual actions of people and their companies. This is where businesses are failing.

Recall Programs

Very few business executives would put Ralph Nader at the top of their list of favorites. But what his consumer movement did was to force businesses to stand behind their products and deliver what they promised. Recall programs are now a way of life—they can be a nuisance, but they are the right way to do business. It is a shame companies could not have done them voluntarily rather than having to succumb to government intervention and threats.

International Integrity

It is estimated that bribes are commonplace in 60% of the countries around the world, especially in underdeveloped countries. The smarter American firms bidding for these contracts refuse to give bribes. Once a company starts to pay bribes, its reputation is known, and the company is continually caught in having to keep up with the game. Corrupt government officials will also take someone else's bribe, making it more competitive and difficult to keep a government contract.

There is increasing national attention over products imported to the United States using child labor in underdeveloped countries for very low wages. The wages paid in some of these countries are extremely fair or even above

> *If you don't stand for something you'll fall for anything!*

the average employment wage in those nations. Through international trade, America's free press and many American businesses will teach America's predominant value system, an ethic derived from The Ten Commandments. In the long run that should help the world's economies come closer to parity—a quality we need to achieve in a world marketplace and serve God's plan.

Your Word

Ken Wessner was a pioneer with ServiceMaster. During his early years of starting contract cleaning in health care businesses, ServiceMaster lacked national credibility and reputation because of its small size and the lack of health of its balance sheet.

After making a presentation to a hospital board, the board asked for Ken's financial statement. A few board members said that they could not use ServiceMaster because its balance sheet was weak. However, a respected board member who knew Ken and his integrity spoke up and said, *I know Ken Wessner and when he gives his word, he will do the job!* Without that meaningful relationship of trust, ServiceMaster would have not had its first big sale, which helped it become a $2 billion management services division employing more than 150,000 people.

Corporate Honesty

Honesty has to start with internal communication within the business, complemented by external communication to the world. Good internal communications includes performance appraisals, fair terminations, forthrightness, communicating with employees a timely way, sharing both the good news and the bad, and meeting customer expectations. These communications are absolutely critical, but too often neglected by executives. Most executives will make the statement to employees, *I don't want any surprises, so if you have any bad news share it with me ahead of time*. The same courtesy should be extended to the employees by top management, who need to seek and reward all types of information given by employees.

Sharing numbers about the business with employees, and training them to interpret and understand their meaning, is an excellent communication tool. It can increase trust, reduce prejudicial comments about performance or productivity, increase a sense of ownership and encourage a sense of responsibility to contribute and perform at a higher level. This is why effective quality programs and *Open Book Management* are effective tools for business.

Negative or Positive?

The information age seems to have created a "media frenzy" to meet the competition for more news, with the addition of more and more cable stations which offer sensational "inside stories" and "talk shows." This frenzy is exposing the public to more and more dishonesty, murder, cheating, violence, adultery, and so on. It's easy for the six o'clock news team to camp at the police station and the court house, to find their shocking, bizarre or murder reports.

As frustrating as this negative news may be to viewers, as we are exposed to moral decay, this can serve God's plan. As evil is exposed and recognized as evil, the exposure creates an opportunity for a cleansing effect . As people repent, ask forgiveness and seek healing, more blessings result.

In truth, these things were happening before the media exposed us to them. Now that they are exposed, we can hope for cleansing and forgiveness. *The negative affect can be those who accept sin as normal.* It requires those who know better to share truth with their fellow man with loving kindness. Notice how truth works through these news stories:

1. A famous baseball player spits in an umpire's face and refuses to apologize. People are outraged, the World Series is delayed, and the story lingers in the media all through the off season. Finally the player apologizes

to the umpire, saying he is sorry, at the first game of the season. The media then drops the story.

2. The Chairman of Chrysler admits that some company officials have become involved in turning back the mileage odometer on executive demonstration cars. He admits the dishonesty was wrong, apologizes, and announces a plan to take action against those involved. The story never makes the news again.

3. The Texaco CEO admits that some executives made the discriminatory remarks about minority employees, and these executives are being fired. The CEO apologizes, settles the law suit brought against Texaco by employees, and creates new procedures for ensuring fair treatment. The story is history within a week.

The Classic Lesson For Us All
. . . Hypocrisy Has A Price

A hypocrite can be referred to as a person who outwardly talks about doing right but privately does what's wrong.

For many of us it's hard to imagine a President of our Country who speaks out against sexual harassment, child abuse, rape, absent fathers, for civil rights, welfare, women's rights and privately forsakes many of the principles these issues stand for.

Nearly all Christians would agree that Jim Bakker and Jimmy Swaggart were hypocrites, who should pay the price for their actions. No different than a CEO caught in an affair and asked to resign by his board.

God has a system to deal with hypocrisy. He starts with forgiveness, (grace), then forgiveness and forgiveness again. At some point after so many wake up calls and opportunities to come clean, He decides that the grace period is over.

President Clinton's bluffing, stalling, lying and denial over his immoral acts require consequences and learning lessons.

It is not by chance that we live in an era of media frenzy, pursuing spectacular stories about "truth and deceit." The President was elected by Americans who overlooked his history and bought into the "popular view" that happiness and fulfillment is about pursuing looks, power, personality, fame, money rather than from integrity, morality and character. Nor is it by chance that He influenced our founders to set up a system for examining and deciding on the fitness of a President to serve. Our Creator wants the truth to be known and Americans to decide who's rules they will follow. It has been a test.

God is again teaching men throughout the world the importance of living by His Truths. The battle is between good and evil, truth and deceit, right and wrong.

The grace period is up and the consequences must be paid.

THE MORAL OF THE STORIES:

1. The poison that can kill good moral works of an individual or company is dishonesty. Honesty may be the highest regarded moral ethic in the American business world.

2. When company executives or employees say one thing but do another, or do nothing (without explanation) their honesty is questioned. Their reputation becomes such that people aren't sure when to believe them, as in the story of Peter and the Wolf. We all need to *walk our talk*.

3. No communication to employees concerning critical events, performance or actions, as well as poor communication is a sin of ommission bordering on dishonesty.

4. Lying is an attempt to control the circumstances of a situation for one's own personal gain. This illustrates pride and self-centered behavior. God is calling us to be God-centered and centered on helping other people— forget yourself and do what is right for others.

5. The future of business is dependent upon the character and morals which your employees bring to your organization, and the character you teach and demonstrate to them. Any employee can kill or rape your business without firing a shot or taking a dime.

How? Simply by dumping key data on a few discs and giving them to people who have bad motives and who desire to harm you or your business.

What Do We Worship?

Gluttony & Addictions. *This usually starts with a habit in seeking pleasure because of a spiritual emptiness that only God can fill. As depression or frustration gets worse, the dependency gets stronger. The addiction provides the temporary high for relief; it becomes a "fix" (or god). The addiction is worshipped and develops destructive control over a person's life. Since the addiction is spiritually rooted, it is impossible for anyone to totally overcome this by his own willpower. Changing the addiction to a dependency on God has the greatest chance to produce a successful turnaround. Besides drugs, alcohol, smoking, and food, there are a number of other addictions people might seek (e.g., work, TV, being a sports fanatic, or even simple things like playing or watching golf, tennis or other sports). Aside from drugs, alcohol and smoking, these other activities do not have to be addictive if kept in proper balance, rather than letting them become an addictive release.*

Movement To And From His Truths

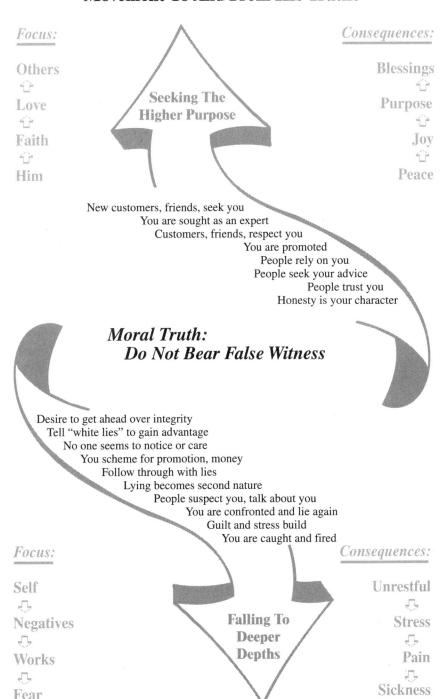

Focus:

Others
⇧
Love
⇧
Faith
⇧
Him

Seeking The Higher Purpose

Consequences:

Blessings
⇧
Purpose
⇧
Joy
⇧
Peace

New customers, friends, seek you
You are sought as an expert
Customers, friends, respect you
You are promoted
People rely on you
People seek your advice
People trust you
Honesty is your character

Moral Truth:
Do Not Bear False Witness

Desire to get ahead over integrity
Tell "white lies" to gain advantage
No one seems to notice or care
You scheme for promotion, money
Follow through with lies
Lying becomes second nature
People suspect you, talk about you
You are confronted and lie again
Guilt and stress build
You are caught and fired

Focus:

Self
⇩
Negatives
⇩
Works
⇩
Fear

Falling To Deeper Depths

Consequences:

Unrestful
⇩
Stress
⇩
Pain
⇩
Sickness

10

DIVERSITY IS A STRENGTH

Moral Truth: *Do not covet.*

Character Quality: *Appreciate and encourage others.*

Trouble Ahead

I'll never forget the day Branch Rickey, former President of the Brooklyn Dodgers, asked me to join his baseball organization. I would be the first Negro to play in organized baseball — that is, if I were good enough to make the grade, said Jackie Robinson. We met in his office on the never-to-be forgotten day when our Marines landed on the soil of Japan, August 29, 1945. From behind his desk the big, powerful, bushy browed Branch Rickey, who seemed a combination of father and boss, mapped out to me his daring strategy to break the color line in major league baseball.

'Mr. Rickey', I said, 'It sounds like a dream come true — not only for me but for my race. For seventy years there has been racial exclusion in big league baseball. There will be trouble ahead — for you, for me, for my people, and for baseball.'

> *Jackie Robinson understood the difference between "I" and "we." He had a higher calling than himself.*
>
> **—Joe Black, Jackie's Dodger roommate**

Rickey picked up on my words by saying 'That's the way it is with most trouble ahead in this world, Jackie — if we use the common sense and courage God gave us, but you have got to study the hazards and build wisely.' He continued, 'God is with us, Jackie. You know your Bible. It's good, simple Christianity for us to face realities and to recognize what we are up against. You can't go out and preach and crusade and bust our heads against the wall. We have got to fight out our problems together with tact and common sense.'

Jackie's first year was with the Montreal Royals Farm Club, where pre-season exhibition games were canceled because of "mixed-race athletes." One of the critical things for Jackie to have to avoid was outbursts of anger which ball players sometimes make over calls or incidents on the field. *I didn't dare lose this way. Many would have dubbed me a 'hothead' and pointed to my outbursts as a reason why Negroes should not play in organized baseball. This is one of the hardest problems I had to face.* That year Montreal won the Junior World Series and Jackie won the batting title with a .349 average. *On April 10, 1947, Branch Rickey made the announcement that gave me my greatest thrill. I joined the Brooklyn Dodgers and became the first Negro to compete in the Major Leagues. I prayed as I never had before.*

Again I faced the same problems as opposing players drove a hard grounder to the infield. When a player crossed first base his spikes bit painfully into my foot. Accident or deliberate, who could tell? But the first reaction of a competitive ball player is to double up his fists and lash out. I was blinding red. It took every bit of my discipline to bridle my temper. When my team mates rushed to my support in white hot anger, it gave me the warmest feeling I have ever felt. At that moment I belonged.

CHARACTER QUALITY

- Appreciate and encourage others -

Covetousness is based on self-centered emotions such as prejudice, jealousy, envy, and bitterness. Caught in a spiritual vacuum, we find comfort in our own *pity party,* blaming others for our hurt. Choosing humility over pride is the key to overcoming covetousness. The Lord knew this would be a problem for us if we don't sincerely work toward being appreciative and encouraging the differences between each of us.

If you were God how would you create people in the world? Would you create everyone the same and give them all the same talents? That would be boring for Him and ourselves. We would all want the same things and be even more apt to fight, disagree and be competitive. Or would you create each of us with talent equal to God's? In that case He would have a big problem...He's the only one who has a right to be jealous, and He isn't looking for any more competition.

He created us all unfinished so that He could have the joy of working through our lives as we call upon Him, and to see us grow and nurture just like parents do with their own child. We all need each other and can support each other because of our different talents. No question—He has a good design.

Can I Come Home?

Johnny Simmons was a young Vietnam soldier returning home. He was sent to Los Angeles before being discharged; from there, he called his mother from a hotel and said, *Mom, I'm back in the States and will be coming home soon.* He also said he had a friend he wanted to bring home with him, but the friend had been badly wounded and lost one eye, an arm and a leg. He asked whether that would be all right.

His mother's voice was hesitant, then she finally said okay, but only for a couple of weeks or less.

A few days later his mother got a call from the L.A. Police Department, reporting that her son was dead. He had jumped from the eighth story of a hotel window. She was told also that her son had only one arm, one leg and one eye.

> *To return evil for good is devilish...*
>
> *To return good for good is neighborly...*
>
> *To return good for evil is God like.*

The Corporate Game

Karen Hanson's story illustrates a situation not uncommon in the politics of corporations. At 22, fresh out of college, Karen was hired by a Fortune 500 Company based in Chicago. She was smart, attractive, and aggressive. Within her first three years she was promoted five times and her vice-president counseled her a number of times about her future career with the company. He was her champion supporter and decided to give her a territory as a sales coordinator in a metropolitan area that was 26th out of all 28 territories.

He was criticized for giving somebody so young such a responsible position but most didn't think too much of it because the territory was considered "a loser." She had one hurdle, however. She had to be approved by the local manager and other staff.

In his interview with her, the manager questioned why she would want this position and told her that she would never make it because she was too young and attractive. But after all the dust settled, the manager decided to give her a try.

Within nine months she had brought the territory production from no. 26 to no. 6. At a corporate-wide meeting she was recognized twice because of the great turnaround in her area. However, many employees she left behind were jealous; they created rumors and criticized the boss behind his back for his decision to promote her. The CEO questioned him as to why she had been promoted so quickly.

A critical spirit is like poison ivy...
It only takes a little contact to spread poison.

From on high, the corporate board decided it was time to cut costs and improve margins, to increase profitability and be able to get the "flat" stock to appreciate more rapidly. So the message came down to consolidate the sales territories, combining Karen's area with one run by a man. Karen was asked to take a lesser position—in disgust, bitterness, and hurt over a series of broken promises, she resigned.

These kinds of true stories are often referred to as the "silent sins" generated by company politics. They fuel internal conflicts, productivity problems and jealousies. They damage morale and keep many companies from reaching their full potential.

Tit-For-Tat

In another case, George Williams was hired from the outside to take over a department which was "misfiring." Within three months he had done an excellent job and seemed to be performing very well. Everyone seemed to be working as a team.

A new CEO was brought in and asked for performance reviews in light of salary increases proposed. Tom was George's direct supervisor and they always seemed to get along with one another, but Tom made the mistake of focusing on two small problems with George on his face-to-face performance review rather than on the big picture and overall evaluation. He then laid out a very small raise for George. There was some bitterness and jealousy between the two that was covered over in the past.

George, like many people, was good at hiding his emotions and hurt, but made a conscious decision that he would get revenge. He took immediate action. He called his former

Case I — How Resentment Builds

Resentment starts

Defensive, getting back

Spreading the word

The word spreads fast.

More resentment is created, barriers are built, productivity hurt!

Case II — Resentment Overcome

Resentment starts

Sincere, forgiving and not defensive.

Spreading the good word

The word spreads fast.

Harmony, openness, caring are fostered.
Productivity increases.

employer to determine whether they might have a job for him, within two weeks he was gone. Tom, holding onto his resentment and pride, was not willing to apologize or make any effort to correct his mistakes, and the CEO did not want to intervene and take away the responsibility he had given Tom.

Productivity in George's department went down and the expensive search to find another person began.

> *Company CEO's spend 90% of their time making their companies look good for investors, not being good. Managers spend their lives making their little department look good, not working for the good of the company.*
>
> **Peter Senge**

Message or Messenger?

Pricie Hanna, of Scott Paper was promoted to the position of staff vice-president for corporate planning at the age of 32. Her boss said, *It is a big job, Pricie, and a tough one, but based on your performance we are confident you can handle it.* Pricie was entering into a new era working with an all male group and thought to herself. *Maybe I'm the token woman.* But she was confident she could handle the job.

Six months later she was called on to make an important proposal for direction of the company. She said, *I launched into my presentation with some very significant recommendations and had barely finished when another vice-president, obviously anxious to have his say, presented his strong opposing views. As he spoke, I could see the other men nodding their heads in silent approval. In the ensuing debate, my efforts to reinstate my opinions fell on deaf ears. It seemed to me that the others had their minds made up ahead of time. A dreadful thought crossed my mind: Is it just my ideas or have these men rejected me?*

Personally, I was devastated. Time and time again, I was allowing myself to imagine all kinds of slights and ill will.

At home one night in frustration I was reviewing corporate reports and finally tossed them on the floor as I felt the anguish of my position. I started thumbing through my Bible for wisdom, comfort or encouragement of some sort. I stumbled onto the Book of Daniel

> *People who try to whittle you down are only trying to reduce you to their size.*

and saw that he had had similar experiences dealing with three different CEOs (kings) but had relied on his Heavenly Father to guide him through his difficulties. His strategy was simple enough. He just prayed three times a day.

I thought, 'If that can work for him, maybe it can work for me. The idea of praying anytime anywhere — even in the company of business associates — was inspiring. Through prayer God could be with me in a close intimate way whenever I felt alone or insecure or shy.'

I concluded, 'Lord, I have put you in charge of my home and now I have put you in charge of my job and my whole life. I felt better about myself, my colleagues and the challenges I faced. I got my eyes off myself and put them on Him. I moved from the hot seat to another promotion but this time God went with me.'

The Grateful Journal:
Developing the Attitude of Gratitude

Oprah Winfrey shares how her perspective on life was changed when she was fifteen years old. She started to keep a Grateful Journal. Each night she lists five things she is grateful for which happened during the day. Oprah says, *If you focus on what you have, you will always see possibilities. If you focus on what you don't have, you will never have enough.*

Are you Dead?

Bill Cosby, in a speech to students at Howard University which recently aired on C-Span, asked the question, *Are you dead?*

Dead people are waiting to get something. America is a bitter place for dead people. You are polluting the society if you are just sitting and complaining.

If you don't want people to judge you, don't judge others. Don't get stereotyped. Get pride in yourself and forget the easy stuff.

— *Stop going to movies that are degrading.*

— *Disassociate yourself with stereotypes, when you don't want people to do it to you.*

— *Don't waste your money on bad music.*

The fight is about progress. You have to have respect and pass it onto your siblings.

You want to hear the music, do the dance, but you have to pay the piper. You can only blame the person responsible and sometimes that is you. You can become our heroes.

Bill Cosby's comments were not just for young people but for the *me* generation that has been bent on picking their own values. The liberal and humanist view is that we don't want to offend anyone by focusing on God's eternal values which are the higher standard for the real wealth in life.

> *If your heart is right, your mind will follow.*

Hating the Boss

Laura Nash in her book, *Believers in Business*, tells the story of Andy, a Christian who was a supervisor in a manufacturing facility. Unfortunately he worked for a boss he did not respect. He said, *I was preoccupied by the injustices I was witnessing and was angered that such behavior was producing bad results for the business.* Those types of feelings hurt Andy and he felt guilty. Even though he did not discredit them, he felt a sense of hatred inside.

At his local church he was involved in a Bible Study group and shared his frustration with his pastor. The pastor asked him to share it confidentially with the other men to give him advice. Andy felt comfort knowing he was not the only one that had had these kinds of anxieties, and the group gave him good counsel as well.

> *Every person should have a special cemetery lot in which to bury the faults of friends and loved ones.*

Andy's conclusion was that, as a Christian, he needed to use his faith and should start praying in love for his boss. That realization was transforming because it was very hard to hate someone you were praying for. Praying for someone is an act of compassion, love and concern. The net effect was a powerful change in his attitude toward his boss. Andy still disagreed with many of his decisions but he no longer was preoccupied with proving his boss wrong. He found the patience to say, *The fate of my career and this man's are in God's hands, not mine.* Quite suddenly one day Andy was promoted over the other man, who was allowed to "retire."

Pray For One Another

Focus on the Family is an international ministry, based in Colorado Springs, founded by Dr. James Dobson who has a worldwide radio show by the same name. Dobson is also a famous author; Focus on the Family has 75 ministries and over $110 million in annual donations.

If you were to visit their organization, you would see something that is unique in internal business operations. The organization's principal goal is to counsel with people and help them through milestones and difficulties. (Isn't that what every business is supposed to do in helping the customer grow and fill their needs?) Often family concerns hinder personal productivity, so each week department staff meetings review personal as well as business goals, while each staff member is encouraged to pray for one another. It may not be the most efficient way to do business, but the bickering or jealousy that occurs in most organizations are not efficient either. By using this method there develops a better appreciation and understanding of differences, and compassion for one another. You can sense a real difference in this organization in commitment toward one another and caring for people.

Walking The Talk

University of Chicago Annual Survey of over 10,000 employees, A Journey into the Heroic Environment (provided by Rob Lebow) asks "what you want from your employer?" These were typical answers:

People Values

• Treat others with uncompromising truth.
• Lavish trust on your associates.
• Mentor unselfishly.
• Be receptive to new ideas, regardless of their origin.
• Take personal risks for the organization's sake.
• Give credit where it's due.
• Do not touch dishonest dollars.
• Put the interests of others before your own.

Notice how closely those align with The Ten Commandments.

No Comparison

Don't look at somebody else's life or position and say I wish I could have that, says Joe Gibbs, former NFL coach. *God has a plan and you are different. I realize now that God was molding me, building my character (during those times of defeat and frustration) and I needed to be made ready to be a head coach. The key is trust Him, that God will work in your favor.*

Contentment

vs. *Covetousness*

Realizing that I already have everything I need for my present happiness.

CHARACTER
TRAINING
INSTITUTE

THE MORAL OF THE STORIES

1. While the poison of dishonesty can kill, the alcohol of coveting and its equivalents slows a business heart rate, with the potential of causing a slow death.

2. Company executives create the opportunities for people to covet, be jealous or envious of others. For example, they can create undue competition for promotion to the top positions in the company. This can create jealousy, bitterness, rumors and resignations. Recognition is good, but only in proper balance. Servant leadership, horizontal management, character training, team recognition and other similar programs help to deal with this more constructively.

3. The bottom line is that coveting, jealousy, envy, bitterness, prejudice and hurt all lessen productivity within the organization and reduce the effectiveness of team work and potential profitability. This is the biggest area of waste in American business.

4. If we hold the words of bitterness, envy, and jealousy within our heart, they turn into weeds, causing discomfort, lack of peace, pain and sickness. That is

> *He who throws dirt loses ground.*

why God said *Do not covet.* He knew how he built the emotional, physical, mental and spiritual parts of our being. Rarely do any of us tell someone else that we hate them, but when we keep the pain of their words in our heart, we suffer every time we see the person. We are the ones who suffer, rather than the person who is hated. Our hatred hurts us far more than it hurts them.

5. The purpose of a business is to be a tool of God, building the character of each of us so that we learn to love, to grow together toward His purposes and to be respectful of different roles, talents, stations and economic circumstances.

What Do We Worship?

Envy *is learned from parents and from the deceit of others. It is a hiding place for a damaged heart. People find comfort in "pity parties," wallowing in the hurt they feel of being deprived and short-changed in life. They become paralyzed in their dreams and desires to have what others have, and allow bitterness to develop into resentment for others. Envy is fueled with gossip and breeds more jealousy and hurt.*

THE DOWNWARD CYCLE

Focused on department interests

Loyal to department concerns

Protective of department needs

Distrusting of "outsiders"

Influenced by rumors and false reports

Committed to erroneous conclusions

Makers of false accusations

Controlled by hidden/open conflict with other departments

Dedicated to internal competition

Drained by energy loss

Burned out by inefficiency

Hampered by lowered productivity/quality

Customer dissatisfaction

Revenue Loss

**From Beyond
the Bottom Line**

THE BODY OF THE COMPANY

We are all created to take on His image.
Everything needs to work together for good to succeed long **term.**

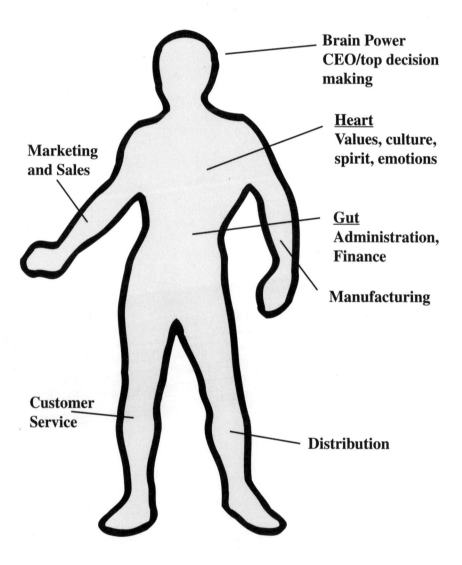

Brain Power
CEO/top decision
making

<u>Heart</u>
Values, culture,
spirit, emotions

**Marketing
and Sales**

<u>Gut</u>
Administration,
Finance

Manufacturing

**Customer
Service**

Distribution

Every body part is different on purpose to function as a unit,
as such, all parts suffer if one part is hurt.

Movement To And From His Truths

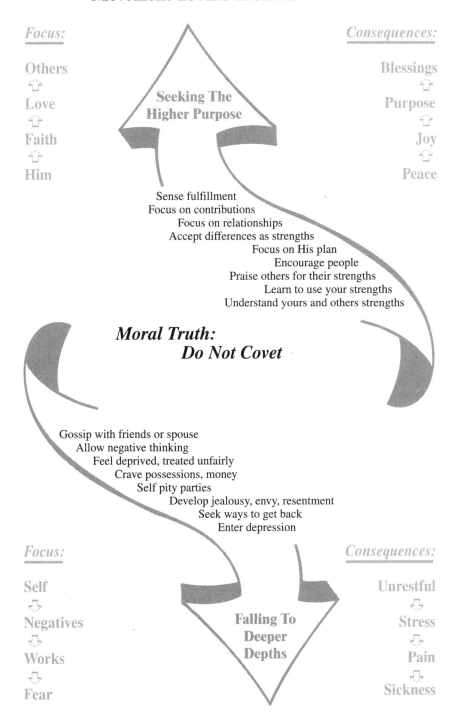

The Life in Death of Princess Diana
Character and Moral Truth
(An Example For The Living)

The world has mourned two great women who have exemplified and embodied the Moral Truths of "Love Your Neighbors as Yourself." Princess Diana and Mother Teresa were given a spirit of compassion for those in need. They spread their unselfish love throughout the world to all ages, in all circumstances.

Princess Diana proved that you can be physically beautiful, motherly, romantic, wealthy, famous, and love the sickest of sick and the poorest of poor. God loved her example because as we love one another, we love Him and live by His Truths.

Why wouldn't God heal Diana on the operating table the night of the car crash? He has used His miracles millions of times before. Was not God sad over her death? Didn't He want her to continue good for the needy and be an example?

God always looks at the greatest good over the long term because He has a plan for the course of human events. God does see death as final because He has an Eternity waiting for righteous servants to be with Him. Yet, God allows some people to die as a sacrifice for those of us who remain on earth. The men and women who have died prematurely in wars, even sickness and accidents serve as a "wake up call" to draw us closer to Him and His purpose.

Funerals say, Why God? and often thank God either can lead to repentance and soul searching in our lives. It reminds us of our own mortality and that we are <u>not</u> in control. It brings us to a deeper conviction to find our purpose, peace, love, and joy in the life we live. The message is that we have to "Let God be God."

The Life in Death of Princess Diana
(Continued)

God understands our emotions and sadness. He gave the greatest gift of all, the life of His son sacrificed for the mistakes of mankind. His life and example have changed the world and allowed God's grace and Holy Spirit to be active in our lives.

We can be a sacrifice in life or death. It is our free choice. Our sacrifice in life is about being a servant to Him and our fellow man—doing his will, not our own.

Mother Teresa's life was a sacrifice _in_ living. Princess Diana's life is a sacrifice _for_ the living. Her eulogy and memory will be replayed every anniversary in all types of media coverage throughout the world.

The 2.5 billion who paid their respects in London or on the record worldwide TV coverage were touched by the Holy Spirit—in a release of warmth, peace, and healing in their loss. We are all touched by her example. Her example brings life through her death. The world is searching for role models to fashion and emulate their character. Already people and organizations are promising to donate or help carry on the work she championed. Just like young men and women who want to grow up like their childhood hero, her efforts will be replicated with even more compassion and strength by many.

Diana's actions and behavior are being savored over her glamour and will change the lives of millions—more in death than in life.

Yet there is an even greater purpose in living found in God's Spiritual Truths, explained in the pages ahead.

Spiritual Truths

The inner core of every human being is a spirit, often referred to as the *heart*. God is The Spirit of *love, truth and light* who communicates with our inner spirit, dependent on our relationship with Him.

The first four commandments of the Ten Commandments call us to be open to His leading. When Jesus was asked what is the greatest commandment of all, He said, Love your Lord God with all your heart, soul and might; *summarizing these four commands in one phrase.*

He wants a personal relationship with each of us, to love us and communicate with us daily. He did not create us to be alone. He wants us to learn His ways and grow closer to the purposes He has for each of us. As we do, His leading and involvement becomes apparent. Unless we keep growing closer to him, we may miss His guiding.

Through visions and insight, He inspires many to start, grow or turn businesses around.

True peace, love and joy can only be found through our spiritual and servant relationship with Him. This is the secret to true wealth in life.

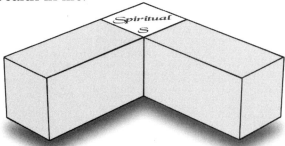

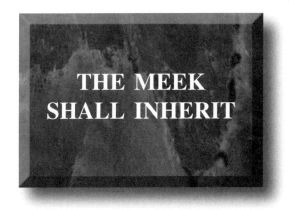

THE MEEK SHALL INHERIT

Spiritual Truth: *Have no other Gods.*

Character Quality: *Be humble and trust Him.*

The Core of the Problem

Coach Bill McCartney describes an incident which illustrates our problem. He had just walked on to the practice field with his players; not 30 minutes later his trainer called across the field and said, *Coach, there is a phone call for you.* McCartney yelled back, *You know I don't take phone calls during practice.* And the trainer yelled back, *Yeah, Coach, but its Sports Illustrated calling.* McCartney thought for a moment or two and finally said, *Okay, I will be there, have him hang on.*

He had to walk all the way across three practice fields, up a large ramp to his office in the stadium. As he walked he started thinking about *What do they want from me? Perhaps they want to write an article to set the records straight about some of the awful things they said about us last year when we won the national championship. Or perhaps they want to write about how we should really be ranked number 1 over two other contenders in the polls.*

As he mulled over in his mind how he would answer these questions, he finally got to his office and picked up the phone. He said hello and the person on the other end said, 'Hello, Mr. McCartney?' He said, 'Yes.' 'This is Sports Illustrated and we needed to call you because your subscription is about to run out."

> *Most people wish to serve God... But only in an advisory capacity.*

As McCartney shares that story, he says it is typical of how self-centered we can become, and how we can place higher importance on ourselves than we deserve.

Never Quit

Many would call John Scott a self-made man. By the time he was 28 years old, he had a retail chain of eight stores and was already a millionaire. Then he encountered some up and down experiences that caused him to revert to his college athletic career and the attitude of *never, never quit.* After he built the business up to 28 different locations, some of his products started to become "commodities" as they were introduced through the discount stores of Wal-Mart and K-Mart. He had to start cutting back and looking for other sources of capital to rebuild. His corporate and personal debt were escalating.

A couple of competitors offered to buy his chain but he declined. After reducing to 12 stores he was offered $5 million; at 6 stores he was offered $3 million, and finally the last offer was $1 million before he was forced to close and liquidate whatever assets remained. John considered himself a Christian and claimed to pray for God's direction. Most of his advisors urged him to sell and get out at each of the stages, but he confused selling with quitting. It is hard for many people to become meek enough to listen and stop being too proud to be right.

CHARACTER QUALITY

- *Be Humble and Trust Him* -

Dr. Laura Nash, author of the book, *Believers in Business*, says that through her interviews with Christian CEOs she learned that *the problem with ego is not with having an ego but with losing one's proper perspective. The problem can be expressed in quantitative terms of excess —thinking too much of one's own ability—or it can be expressed in terms of relationships. Hyperinflated self-regard contributes to a broken relationship with God and with one's neighbor.*

Dean Sherman asks the question, *Are you a horse, mule, or sheep?* Sometimes to get the attention of a horse you have to slap him up the side of the head, and with a mule it is typical to use a 2 x 4, but a sheep is a good follower. The Lord does not want us to lose our aggressiveness or willingness to take risks, but He also wants us to be as meek as sheep to listen and be used by Him and our fellowman. The plan is for us to be servants, not kings.

Being our Creator, omnipotent and invisible, allows Him to work through us in ways that we can't totally fathom. Two things bother Him significantly: arrogance and ignorance—yet He is incredibly tolerant with us for long periods of time.

The first commandment, having *no other Gods before Him*, becomes our most pivotal choice and affects every other relationship and attitude throughout our entire life.

The question is whether we are so "prideful" in our own success or accomplishments that we don't need any other god besides ourselves— we are in total control and fear losing it. Life's character lessons get our attention, if we just allow ourselves to be humble and trust Him.

Being Open

In the late 1960s, Charles Smith was forced to take over as CEO of a struggling $30 million company; but through his determination, financial savvy and openness he parlayed the company into a $2 billion conglomerate. With national publicity and recognition, he was considered a highly respected and sought-after CEO. He was befriended by another corporate head who had his own $2 billion company but was seeking to retire and phase out. He persuaded Charles to buy his personal stock and come on his board as he transitioned out.

Charles was advised by friends and business associates not to buy, but his businesses had gone through twelve years of 47% compounded growth, and he saw great potential in this corporation. He had stopped listening and felt invincible; over their objections, he bought the company. Unfortunately, what he had not visualized was a coming recession and that his friend had not laid out all the facts nor been totally open and honest with him. Within a year Charles, as the director with the most experience, was forced to take over as CEO and turn the company around. Because of the financial leverage he had used to buy the new business, results were disastrous for the company he built as well as for the company he acquired.

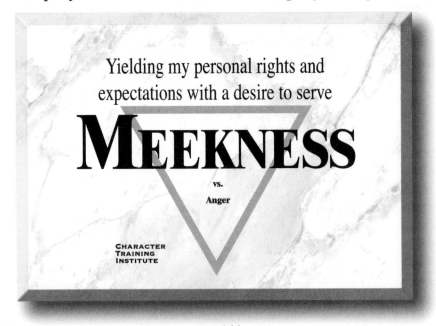

Yielding my personal rights and expectations with a desire to serve

MEEKNESS

vs.

Anger

CHARACTER
TRAINING
INSTITUTE

Today he wishes he had listened to those who were giving him wise counsel. His personal assets went from $60 million to $10 million—a big lesson learned.

The Abundant Life

Wes Cantrell started his business career with Lanier in Atlanta before being transferred to Baton Rouge. After stops along the way in Gulfport and Augusta, he was back in Baton Rouge in 1961 as District Manager.

Don't trust yourself to be your own god.

The transition from sales to management was a tough one, and he struggled. At twenty-seven, he had never worked in an office with another person. Some of the employees he inherited had a goal to undermine his leadership. Within a few months, it was obvious to him that he was failing. He struggled with what he should do to turn himself around.

After Wes returned from a trip, his wife suggested they go to revival at their church. That night, Mike Gilchrist preached a sermon which he entitled "Heaven on Earth," about the spirit-filled life which is promised in the Scriptures. It was new to Wes. Even as a preacher's son, he could not remember ever hearing this message before.

The message that night spoke to his heart as he sincerely committed himself to be a Christian and asked that the Holy Spirit would come and dwell within him, within his own spirit. He wanted the beginning of an abundant life right away.

Wes believed that God had a plan for his whole life, and he wanted God to be involved in every aspect—business, family and social. Wes had separated his life into compartments: thorough the week as district manager, weekends as deacon and Sunday School teachers, and at home as father and husband. With this teaching, he began to understand that God had a will and purpose in all aspects of his life, and that, if he would follow God, he could truly experience an abundant life.

Both Wes and his wife, Bernadine, had already committed their lives to Christ, but this experience and insight brought them to a deeper faith and a walk with real expectations.

Immediately, Wes began to apply his faith to his business. He relaxed and believed that if God wanted him to stay in the same job, he would be successful. If not, it was His sure way of telling Wes that He had plans for him somewhere else. Wes didn't change his diligence, determination or work ethic. This time, though, it was the Lord who was his real boss.

Amazing things began to happen. It was as if you could draw a line *before* and *after*. The business began to turn around. He made some tough decisions. He fired the troublemaker in his office, even though he was top salesman in the company. God brought in some wonderful new people who became very productive, and the office began to flourish. The morale in the office simply soared. In a short period of time, it became Lanier's top office with sales increases that caused the business to double the last two years he was manager. It was obvious to Wes that God wanted him in Baton Rouge, and made him successful.

Shortly thereafter, he received the most important promotion in his career—to head up all of Lanier's dictation product sales in 1996. Wes shared, *There is no question in my mind that my decision to be filled with the Spirit and to allow God to have His way in my life led to all these wonderful things. At that time, Lanier was $12 million annually. Today, Lanier is a $1.2 billion company. Through all these years, it has been my objective to allow God to have His way in my life, which includes now my family, my business, my church and my community. Praise the Lord for giving us the abundant life!*

> *Many CEOs go broke because they won't subject their ideas for possible criticism.*
>
> **Brian Tracey**

The Control Factor

Of all the ways we become deceived,
the most critical is our fixation with
looking good. We believe we have to be in
control. We don't want to look stupid in the
eyes of other people, a fear perpetuated
throughout our society.

The bottom line is that there is only one
person in control—the one who created us. No
matter what we think we have done on our own,
He has been available to help, according on His
purpose and plan.

We can work with Him or against Him.
Life is just much more peaceful
and wealth if we surrender to
His control.

The Invincible Giant

For years IBM has been considered to be the No. 1 Blue Chip company in the United States. It seems to have set the tone for professionalism, management, training and credibility. Unfortunately, the egotism and pride of key executives impaired their vision and listening skills. The company that had made a promise never to lay anyone off went from 420,000 employees down to 200,000 over twelve years.

The customer was telling the corporate giant that the market was moving away from main frame computers to the personal computers (PC's) for everyday use in most businesses. They passed up early opportunities to be the leader in that segment as well as the software industry. Unfortunately, many of the top executives had been entrenched in "Big Blue" corporate pride, high salaries and bureaucracy, unable to listen to and change with the marketplace.

IBM is rebounding with new and fresh outside leadership. Maybe they will be humble enough to listen.

The same kind of wake-up bell rang in the 1970s and 1980s for the auto industry, when the oil crises pointed toward building more fuel-efficient cars. However, their arrogance prevented car companies from hearing the first bell, and the Japanese and Germans stole a major portion of their market share while they refused to listen and take action.

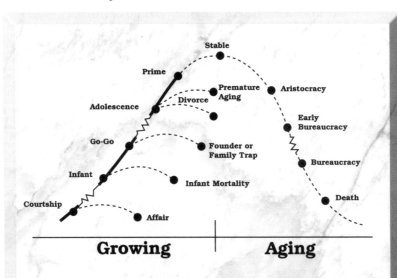

Ichak Adizes, PhD., in researching his book *Corporate Lifecycles: How and Why Corporations Grow and Die and What to Do about It*, discovered the patterns of success and failure. These patterns apply to businesses of all sizes. Once new businesses have made it past the "go-go" stage, egotism among top executives starts to set in. Humility, not egotism, remains the key to successfully listening and focusing on customers. God works through the customer, telling executives to listen with their heart as well as their soul. IBM and many other notable examples have gotten their "wake-up call" as they struggled to break out of the downturn cycles by going back to the basics of listening in humility.

Egotism

Tom Phillips, former chairman of Raytheon, says that ego is the number one cause of business mistakes. He relates, *In most take over situations, the CEO goes to his board initially with incomplete information—by necessity. They recommend an offer, and only then are all the financials available. At* that point it is almost impossible for a CEO to change his recommendation. His ego is on the line. It was his project, and yet that is precisely the point when a good leader must have the ability to say, 'that is not such a good deal after all.'

> *He wants men great enough to be small enough to be used.*

Wisdom

God seeks humble, obedient listeners and followers, people led by His Spirit to unfold His plans. This is evidenced by many Christians who, when asked to do something may say, *Let me pray about it to seek His confirmation.*

If we will not be humble before God, eventually our unwillingness to listen takes its toll and we become humble through the school of hard knocks.

Getting "Buy In"

Richard Hagberg, the noted California consultant who specializes in working with high growth firms in the Silicon Valley, says that *Typically CEOs are good at developing a vision, which they think they have communicated, but frequently their strategy is not*

> *My number one job is to please God.*
> **Bobby Bowden**

widely understood. Their impatience drives them to focus on financial goals, which means they fail to build relationships with boards or their employees.

When CEOs lose touch with their employees and they become isolated, they think they have 'buy in' but what they have is false consensus. They are far less effective in facilitating team work and gainful participation than they are in decision making.

> *You should never let adversity get you down... Except on your knees.*

If they see themselves as too self-important, they will be defensive because they have a vested interest in maintaining an image of themselves as omnipotent. And that can be an absolute killer.

God Inspired

During the middle of the gas crisis in the mid-1970s, a humble businessman by the name of Bob Harrison believed that God was leading him to buy a Chrysler dealership. It seemed crazy and illogical to him. People were turning in their gas guzzling cars as fast as they could, and Chrysler, which made virtually no economy cars, was in a tailspin and had run out of capital. But he confirmed the leading of his heart with wise business counsel and bought a Southern California dealership, including its inventory, for less than $50,000 down. Within ninety days it was one of the ten top dealerships in sales in Southern California. Years later, Bob and his family sold the dealership and moved on to teach other businessmen about the Biblical concepts that he learned in being humble and listening to his God.

> *People with humility don't think less of themselves, they just think of themselves less.*
>
> **Ken Blanchard**

Hurricane Faith

Fresh out of school, starting as the secretary to the President of Southeastern Metals was a traumatic experience for young Nadine Gramling, but she learned quickly and became Sales Manager and then President, taking the company from $10 million in sales to $90 million.

She always shared her faith with her employees through her walk, but one day her faith was severely tested. After Hurricane Andrew, South Florida officials did a reassessment of their construction codes, and investigative reporters singled out her company as being under standard.

For nearly four weeks the media was "in her face" in preparation for the county's testing of her metal roofing products. The danger was that if they failed the test, the company could be open for lawsuits and her distributors would drop their products. She said, *We could have lost the whole company. I was not in control. I was involved in a circumstance I had never been prepared to face before. I turned to God and never prayed so hard in my entire life.*

The outdoor test was with a wooden 2x4 shot twice from a cannon. It rained and the wood was twice as heavy as normal,

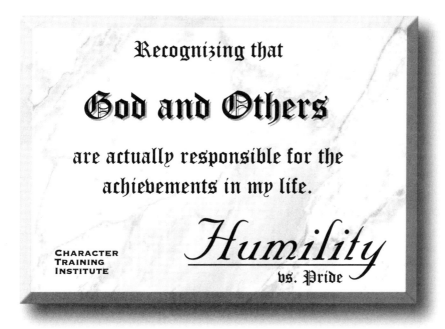

Recognizing that

God and Others

are actually responsible for the achievements in my life.

CHARACTER TRAINING INSTITUTE

Humility

vs. Pride

> *Egotism is the only disease known to man that seems to make everybody sick... except the carrier.*
>
> **Charles "Red" Scott**

leaving the margin of error only 1 / 16 of an inch, but by the time of the test, she had received real peace of mind.

She concluded, *We passed with flying colors only because of the grace of God. We were put under unfair circumstances and conditions. Only God could have pulled us through. He made the difference.*

Kitchen Table Shoemaker

In the mid-1950s Bob Bowerman was a track coach at the University of Oregon. He was constantly frustrated with the injuries of his athletes. He attributed many of their problems to the shoes typically sold to track athletes. He began work on different ideas and concepts at his kitchen table, until he designed a new shoe that would be lighter, more comfortable and more flexible. He tried to sell his concept to companies without success. Eventually he became totally discouraged.

One day in attempting to encourage his team he quoted the apostle Paul: *Do you not know that in a race all the runners run, but only one gets the prize? Run in such a way as to get the prize.* (I Corinthians 9:24). He explained that winning is important, but it's not the only goal. Later he realized that same advice applied to his life. It was as if God was saying to keep on running, to persevere, and that somehow he would get those shoes made, even if he had to do it himself.

So he hand-crafted a pair of shoes on his kitchen table and asked some of his runners to try them out. Their response was very encouraging. His miler, Phil Knight, became very enthusiastic about the shoes. After graduating from Stanford, Phil found shoe manufacturers and distributors interested in the shoes and developed a unique marketing concept. Little did Bob or Phil know that they were creating a whole new industry. They picked the name "Nike" for their company. The rest is history.

Listening For A Small Voice

James Kraft, the founder of Kraft Foods, peddled his cheese from a horse-drawn wagon during the early days. At one point, he became very discouraged because sales were poor and his capital was exhausted. He saw himself as a failure.

> *God opposes the proud but gives grace to the humble.*
> **1 Peter 5:5**

One day he just stopped in total despair. He said, *For the moment my mind was clear of frantic planning and thinking. It was a receptive interlude. And at that moment it came to me, clearly and distinctly, this conviction: 'You have been working without God.'*

I stopped to listen. For the first time in my life I had been able to hear the words which must have been spoken to the deaf ears of all of us over and over again. I resolved to let God have direction in my life. And from that moment forward, my life began to change in every way. Defeat was impossible — because I had been given an 'invincible asset.' I have never stopped listening since.

James Kraft's business became a phenomenal success, and he became a great spokesman for the power of God working in one's life. He said, *In the stillness of spirit, a man is of listening heart and mind. He is conditioned spiritually for divine guidance. The second, and most direct route to inspiration, is the daily systematic habit of reading the Word of God. It speaks directly to men and women — powerfully, and personally. Daily reading the Bible, I am convinced, prepares the man and the heart for hearing the will of God.*

The third and safest, surest and swiftest road to victory is prayer — the habit of prayer which was once the familiar, everyday blessing that it was intended to be in this nation. Personal and family prayer, practiced daily in quietness of spirit, could, I believe, alter the whole world, as I know it alters individual lives.

> *The main requirements of leadership are guts and judgment. To win trust you have to make yourself vulnerable.*
> **Michael H. Walsh CEO, Tenneco**

THE MORAL OF THE STORIES:

1. *Have no other Gods before me* is about being teachable and open, listening and seeking, being humble and trusting Him. He can speak to our heart directly, or He can use other people, creating and allowing circumstances which ultimately get our attention. Those with wisdom seek Him.

2. Financial success or receiving an inheritance can lead to false confidence, pride, and egotism. It is the self-made man or woman's attitude *I am my own person* that will not hold up for a lifetime, let alone for eternity. We either choose to be humble before God, or He allows the weight of our own arrogance to create pain which will lead to humility.

3. The greatest intimidation for too many is that we will lose control or look stupid in the eyes of other people. That is why it is important to trust God because there is no way humanly possible for us to live a full, peaceful and joyous life with this anguish looming over us. No matter what we do, there will be times we lose control and look stupid, but it's okay, we can be forgiven. Estimates are that 92% of the time we are not in control of our circumstances.

What is Being Saved?
(The Eternal Aspects of Success)

It is a state of love and forgiveness that God freely gives us, when we sincerely surrender to his leading. He is holy, and we are not, because we are part of a world off course from His intent. He seeks a personal relationship that allows Him to cleanse our spirit, and live through us and assure us a place in Heaven.

We are saved from the lies, mistakes, pressures and lack of understanding with which missing the mark (sin) tries to grip us. We enter a state of grace that opens the door to a more fulfilling and loving life. Do we sin again? Probably, but as we seek His forgiveness, it is forgotten. Being saved is the beginning of an eternal journey that leads to His plan for our success.

4. He wants to be the God of everyday, not the God of last resort. He wants a personal daily relationship where we walk and talk together and He has an opportunity to love us as He intended and for us to love Him in return.

5. He created us and intimately knows us and our every need. But He wants to be asked to enter our life and lead us to greater success.

6. Yes, we need to be concerned about ourselves with good planning, initiative, follow through, and confidence; but not to the point of worry. The more self-centered we become, the more we worry about ourselves. He wants us to be God-centered and centered toward the interests of our fellowman. No where in the Bible does it say to focus on your self esteem.

7. The vision for truly long-term successful businesses and organizations always comes from God working through people who are humble enough to receive the *vision* he puts on their heart.

8. Suicide is a self-centered act. Sacrifice is an inspiration and learning experience shared with others.

What Do We Worship?

Pride and Egotism are based on a belief in one's self to the point of saying such things as, **'Whatever I earn I get; I'm number one; I am a self-made man/woman; I can be anything I want to be; I am woman, and I am strong, and I control my own destiny; I am my own man, and I did it my way.'** Being proud of your family, business and friends is fine. Being proud without recognizing God and His blessings upon you shows a lack of knowledge. He created each of us. If we use our God-given talents to get ahead or to become successful without sincerely thanking Him for those talents, we are blinded by deceit. We have, in effect, chosen to say, I'm my own god. Typically we are self-centered, concerned about being right (having all the right answers), wanting always to be in control, or looking good, and we get defensive when challenged or when someone defies us, wanting to prove ourselves right.. All these are characteristics of pride gone too far. It is either arrogance or ignorance, apart from God.

Movement To And From His Truths

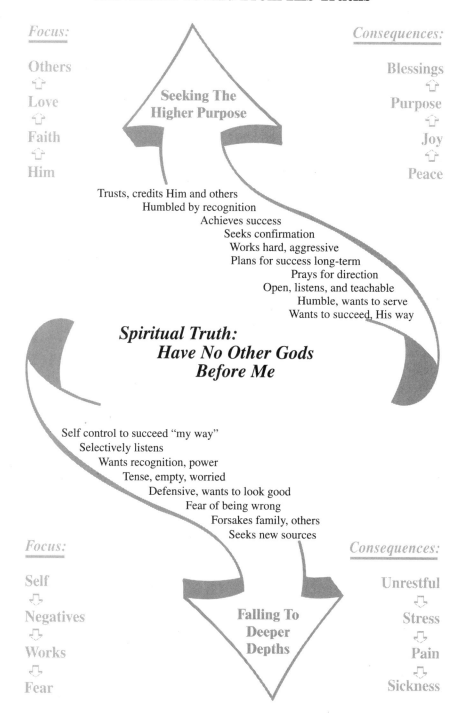

Focus:

Others
⇧
Love
⇧
Faith
⇧
Him

Seeking The Higher Purpose

Consequences:

Blessings
⇧
Purpose
⇧
Joy
⇧
Peace

Trusts, credits Him and others
Humbled by recognition
Achieves success
Seeks confirmation
Works hard, aggressive
Plans for success long-term
Prays for direction
Open, listens, and teachable
Humble, wants to serve
Wants to succeed, His way

Spiritual Truth:
Have No Other Gods
Before Me

Self control to succeed "my way"
Selectively listens
Wants recognition, power
Tense, empty, worried
Defensive, wants to look good
Fear of being wrong
Forsakes family, others
Seeks new sources

Focus:

Self
⇩
Negatives
⇩
Works
⇩
Fear

Falling To Deeper Depths

Consequences:

Unrestful
⇩
Stress
⇩
Pain
⇩
Sickness

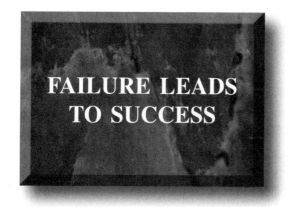

FAILURE LEADS TO SUCCESS

Spiritual Truth: *Have no false idols.*

Character Quality: *Be convicted and forgiven.*

Heartbreak Can Open New Doors

Mary Kay worked eleven years for a national direct sales company as the national training director. With 1,500 women to oversee throughout the country, she was constantly traveling. Company sales were flat. and turnover was high. She urged the top executive to give her help to be able to cover more territory and give the sales people the tools and encouragement to increase sales and profits. Her constant urgings fell on deaf ears.

Finally, the Chief Executive decided to hire an assistant whom Mary Kay would train. Elated, she did her best to coach and train the man. It allowed her to cut down on her travel and be involved in other aspects of increasing sales.

> *Experience is what you get when you don't get what you want.*

Within a year the Chief Executive promoted this new individual over her to national sales manager (at twice the salary), a position she was already performing without the title. When she heard the news, she went home and cried her heart out. She wrote a letter of resignation and never heard from the company again.

Little did this company know that Mary Kay was a woman of destiny and that God had a greater plan for her. She made no efforts to file a discrimination case but decided that she was going to encourage other women to get involved in the business world. She decided to write a book but as she laid out the qualities of her "dream company," she felt convicted that she was being called to build a company that represents the ideals and principles that she believed and wanted to share with others. Today her company approaches nearly $2 billion in sales with over 400,000 distributors.

Conviction Overcomes Defeat

Few great leaders encounter defeat so consistently before enjoying ultimate victory, as did this individual. A frequently reported listing of these failures include the following:

- Failed in business in 1831.
- Ran for the legislature and lost in 1832.
- Failed once in business in 1834.
- Sweetheart died in 1835.
- Had a nervous breakdown in 1836.
- Lost a second political race in 1838.
- Defeated for Congress in 1843.
- Defeated for Congress in 1846.
- Defeated for Congress in 1848.
- Defeated for the Senate in 1855.
- Defeated for Vice-President in 1856.
- Defeated for the Senate in 1858.

The man was Abraham Lincoln, elected 16th President of the United States in 1860.

CHARACTER QUALITY

- Be Convicted and Forgiven -

As long as man and woman have existed on earth they have sought a god to worship. In the days of the Old Testament many created statues, golden calves, or other idols, while others worshipped the sun, the wind and/or the earth and called them gods.

In American society, founded on Christian Biblical principles, we have experienced the greatest prosperity in the shortest period of time of any other nation on earth. However, many of us are:

1. Too intelligent to fall for a "story of a savior dying on a cross."

2. Too complacent, prosperous or satisfied to care (believing that this is the way the good life is supposed to be).

3. Too hopelessly blinded by deceit and lust to understand.

Most of us have chosen a variety of *false idols* to worship, to fill the spiritual void in our lives. The Bible refers to these in different passages and they are most often recognized as the "Seven Sins of the Heart," caused from habits, bondage, inheritance or curse. They are pride/egotism, laziness, envy, greed, addictions, anger and lust. These false idols create a situation of trying to serve two masters. God knew it wouldn't work and that is why He told us to only worship Him.

Some people have to be fired, others end up in a hospital or lose a loved one before their "wake-up" call creates the humility and conviction He is waiting to see. He is ready to forgive us and love us, if we just have the faith to seek Him.

Failure can be a real "God-sent" experience that has a meaningful purpose for our lives.

The Rightful Owner

Kell Williams, II is President of a very successful $100 million company, near St. Petersburg, which produces culverts for road construction. He is highly respected by his peers as a successful business executive.

Kell tells the story of how he went through a very difficult time a few years ago. Company sales dropped by nearly 30%, and they were losing a lot of money, no matter what Kell did. Since the industry was also down, he just could not believe the pressure it put him under. He had many sleepless nights and was afraid to talk honestly to anyone about it.

Success is never permanent, failure is never fatal.

Finally one night he just couldn't sleep, and got out of bed, got on his hands and knees, and said, *Lord, I know this is your business. You led me into it, but I just can't take the pressure anymore. What I am doing is not working. If you want to see it survive and be successful, then it is up to you.*

He contended that night was the turning point in lifting the pressure from his shoulders. He had tremendous peace come over him. He finally got up the nerve to share his difficulties more openly with his CEO advisory group. The business turned around, but while sales never matched their highest levels, his profits dramatically improved. He enjoys telling me this story because he can give God the credit.

A Second Chance

Alfred Nobel was a Swedish chemist who had great success in developing explosives used in a number of wars. He had become wealthy from his success. One day his brother passed away, and the local newspaper wrote an obituary mistaking Alfred for his brother. The obituary described Alfred as a man who became rich by enabling people to kill each other in unprecedented numbers. Shaken by this assessment, Nobel resolved to use his fortune to honor the accomplishments of humanity rather than focusing on destruction. He then created the Nobel Peace Prize,

To know God's will, things often have to get worse until He knows you are ready.

which recognizes several men and women throughout the world each year for their peaceful contributions to mankind.

Not Fit for Television

When she was growing up in Mississippi, she would watch her grandmother wash clothes and believed that, even though she was black and female, her life would be better. Speaking to Wellesley College graduates, she said,

My secret to success is that there is a power greater than myself which rules my life. In life, as in all your endeavors (both the good times and the hard times), if you can be still long enough and commit yourself to the force I call God and allow this energy to be connected to your personality, anything is possible. I'm proof of that—not that I'm special—but that anything is possible.

Discernment

vs. judgement

The ability to determine the difference between truth and deceit.

CHARACTER
TRAINING
INSTITUTE

> *The way to succeed is to double your failure rate.*
>
> **Thomas J. Watson**

As a newsperson in Baltimore, she was taken off the air and told she was "not fit for television." She was demoted to a talk show . . . *and it felt like breathing. Doing your passion feels so natural.* What was perceived as a failure became a talk show career that's turned out pretty well for Oprah Winfrey.

Open Book Management

Jack Stack, CEO of Springfield Remanufacturing Corporation ($200 million in sales) and author of the book, *The Great Game of Business*, by necessity forged a new business concept known as *Open Book Management* which many companies are attempting to grasp and implement today. But Jack's early life was a series of failures. As a child, he was such a problem his father was convinced that becoming a priest would change him. After being kicked out of seminary, his father sent him to reform school. After being kicked out again, Jack was convinced that going into the military would please his father, but he was rejected by the military for physical reasons. He finally got a job sweeping floors for his father's company.

By attending night school, he eventually graduated from college and worked his way up the corporate ladder to become the plant manager of a division of International Harvester in Springfield, Missouri. In the midst of International Harvester's decline, Jack and other key executives wanted to "save their jobs" and proceeded to go to 54 banks before they finally arranged the financing to buy their division through one of the highest leveraged buy-outs in history ($100,000 down for a $9 million loan). Jack kept his faith and learned through each rejection. Today his business is considered one of the most innovative companies in America.

Pat Kelly, CEO of Physician Sales and Service, was raised in an orphanage and only saw his father twice after age six. His firing by a firm in Houston led him to start a new business with two partners that today represents one of the fastest growing companies in the United States, with sales of $700 million in just 14 years.

Neither of these men were educated at Harvard. Their failures created humility and openness. Their convictions, determination and unique insights in business led them to further define *Open Book Management* which closely aligns with principles of God's Moral Truths

> *People are not remembered by how few times they fail, but by how often they succeed. Every wrong step is another step forward.*
>
> **Thomas Edison**

Open to the Vision

Ray Kroc, in his early years, dropped out of high school to play the piano in nightclubs and sell paper cups for a living. He even tried his hand (unsuccessfully) at investing in Florida real estate. After serving in World War II, he came home and acquired the national marketing rights for multi-mixers to make milk shakes. His principal customers were drugstores, and as America moved into the suburbs in the 1950s, the drugstores became self-service and dropped their fountain service. His business was failing.

He had heard of the McDonald brothers in San Bernardino, California, who sold 20,000 shakes a month using his equipment. The McDonald brothers had dropped their "car hops" to become the truly first "fast-food," self-serve restaurant with no frills. Their success had received some national attention, and they had tried to franchise the concept, but with no success.

Ray Kroc visited their operation with the intent of encouraging them to expand so he could sell them more mixers. He spent all morning observing their operation from the parking lot. Mobs of people stood in line at lunch time to buy the 15 cent hamburgers, 10 cent fries and 15 cent shakes. After the crowd cleared, he introduced himself to the brothers and said, *My God, I've been standing out there looking at it but I could not believe it. I've got to become involved in this.*

He encouraged the McDonald brothers to find a new franchising agent to open more locations, but frankly they didn't want the travel or headaches. So only a few weeks later he called back to see whether they had found a new agent. When they said *no*, he said he wanted to be that agent. The rest is history (he eventually gave up on his mixer business).

Ray Kroc said, *It was life or death for me.* He became humble and open enough to allow God to place a vision on his heart that has become the model for business success and franchising worldwide. Walt Disney also went through a personal financial crisis before he started calling his mouse *Mickey.* Colonel Sanders was living in near poverty until he started to sell his special recipe for Kentucky Fried Chicken.

> *Human beings, like chickens, thrive best when they have to scratch for what they get.*

Failure breaks our pride and allows us to become humble enough for our spirit to listen to Him, and receive a new direction in our lives.

There is a Purpose

Bobby Bowden, head football coach at Florida State University, says, *Here are two things that happened to me that shaped my career. When they happened I thought they were the worst things that ever happened to me. The first was when I was 13 years old. I was raised in a house that backed up to the high school football field. I could always hear the ball being kicked. That year I was hit with a disease that kept me in bed all year long. I thought that it was the worst thing that could have happened to me.*

My doctor had told me I would never play again. One day, my mom said to me, 'Bobby, do you believe in prayer?' I said, 'Yes, ma'am.' She said, 'Why don't you ask God to heal you?' I did and He did. That year in bed I learned to develop faith. It changed my life.

The second thing was when I was a junior in high school in Birmingham. In practice, I broke my thumb. I continued to play but it got worse and worse. One day after school, I went to the doctor and he put it in a cast and my season was over. My coach said, 'Maybe I can get you another year of eligibility if you drop out of school now and we might get you a college scholarship.' My mom and dad agreed and I worked at home that year and gained 20 pounds (to 150) and got a scholarship. God used those experiences to develop my character, attitude, and faith and shaped the way I would go.

The Source of Visions

Visions don't come from committees; they come to individuals. Some call it their "gut," others their intuition. It comes from the heart through the emotions of our spirit (whether for good or evil, depending on the emotional garden of our heart). The strength of committees is to think logically using their experiences, knowledge and judgment. While visions see beyond logic into the future, most visions die in the battleground of the mind without capturing the imagination of others. Some are merely training for future receptivity of the vision that will become reality in the marketplace and affect thousands of lives.

God is the giver of visions for His long-term purposes. Godly visions come in time of humility, searching and openness. There can be no gods or false idols before us. Ray Kroc sat in the parking lot that morning in San Bernardino, a humble man who saw a vision that the McDonald brothers could not see or lacked emotions or were too tired to pursue. Their logic had gotten the best of them. God needed a man like Ray Kroc, J.C. Penney, Tom Watson, and millions of others whose heart was bigger than their head.

Wake-Up Calls

Here are examples of *wake-up calls* which should cause us to turn to God and look for spiritual direction in our seeking His love.

PERSONAL	BUSINESS
Fight with your spouse	Losing money
Harm to a spouse or child	Poor performance review
Feeling of emptiness	No raise
Tension	Being let go
Death in the family	Passed over for promotion
Fear of negatives	Boss is hard to work with
Divorce	Company closes
Economic pressures	Verbal attacks by others
Relocation	Losing your temper
Added responsibilities	Jealousy and hate
Addictions	Violence

The world is full of the tensions and problems that can create these circumstances, particularly if He is not protecting us. If we continue in the negatives, we have missed one or more of His truths. There are consequences for our actions. They may not be as immediate as we might expect, but in God's timing and mercy He can use these experiences. He is waiting for us to call on His name.

The Spirit of St. Louis

Charles Lindbergh was a brash, energetic and confident risk-taker who had a passion to be the first man to fly from New York to Paris. Two groups of men had tried and failed just months before his 1928 flight. However, a group of St. Louis businessmen believed in Lindbergh enough to back him financially.

God seldom picks the most qualified or best educated but brings us to humbleness... open, teachable and willing to serve.

They helped him find a manufacturer of custom airplanes named Ryan Aircraft, in San Diego. After Lindbergh had been turned down by a New York company which felt he was too inexperienced to fly their plane across the Atlantic Ocean.

The businessmen picked the name "The Spirit of St. Louis" because of their faith in Lindbergh. Being turned down by the New York company opened the door for Lindbergh to work hand-in-hand with the San Diego firm custom design and build the plane for the projected 40-hour flight.

Lindbergh recalled telling his friend, a priest, that he didn't need God. He believed that all he needed for success was a good instrument panel, engine and landing gear. *If it isn't physical, and I can't see it, it isn't real,* Lindbergh declared. Nevertheless, his friend sent him a St. Christopher's medal to take on his flight. Lindbergh rejected the medal.

Before talking off at 5 AM, Lindbergh needed a little mirror to fasten to his instrument panel to help him read a gauge behind him, so he would not need to turn his head. He asked if anyone in the crowd gathered to see him take off had a little mirror he could use. A woman stepped forward to volunteer her pocket mirror. He asked her why she had waited all night in the rain to see him off, and she replied that if she hadn't, he wouldn't have gotten the mirror he needed.

Both the St. Christopher medal and the mirror played significant roles in Lindbergh's journey. His friend stuck the medal in with the brown-bagged sandwich Lindbergh took with him. Half-way through the flight, when Lindbergh was beginning to lose confidence and struggling, he discovered

> *Don't be afraid of pressure. Remember that pressure is what turns a lump of coal into a diamond.*

the medal and hung it on the instrument panel as a source of inspiration, to remind him that God was with him.

Not far from Ireland, Lindbergh fell asleep, causing the plane to go into a circling tail spin. The mirror reflected the sun onto his face so intensely that he woke up from the burning pain—just in time to pull the plane out of the tailspin before he crashed into the ocean.

The joy of reaching Ireland brought Lindbergh new enthusiasm. But by nightfall, when he reached Paris, he struggled to find the airfield. The blinding spotlights from the waiting crowd and his utter exhaustion seemed to freeze his ability to maneuver the plane into a safe landing. Finally he cried out, *"God help me!"* and miraculously the plane descended to a safe landing while 200,000 people wildly greeted him.

What are You Here to Teach Me?

When she has a down experience, Oprah Winfrey says, *Okay, what are you here to teach me?* Her advice for graduates:

Live your life from truth and you will survive everything. You will be wounded many times in life with failures and mistakes. Turn your wounds into wisdom. I have learned that failure is God's way of saying *'excuse me, you are moving in the wrong direction.'*

Try to allow yourself to listen to God on the whisper before the earthquake comes. The whisper is always followed by a little louder voice, then you get a brick, then a brick wall, then the earthquake hits.

The Right God

The late Pete Maravich, a great basketball star, said, *I didn't want a crutch. I saw Christianity in just that way. My God was basketball. I had power, fame, 60 records, and my own Lear jet. I did 'show time' for thousands of people. Yet I was an alcoholic and into cults. I had everything that a 'successful' person supposedly wanted.*

Then one night I went to bed and I couldn't sleep. Every sin in my life came up. At 6:00 in the mor ning an angel said to me, 'be strong in Him in thine own heart, God still loves you, you can still come home.' My life has not been the same since.

The Gift of Watergate

Chuck Colson, former chief counsel to President Nixon, says, *Life is a paradox. I thank God for Watergate because I learned the greatest lessons of my life. The teachings of Jesus are true. 'He who seeks to save his life will lose it, he who loses his life for My sake will find it.'* (Matthew 16:25).

At 39 I was a successful attor ney and asked to join the White House as Special Counsel to President Nixon. I had achieved what my dad told me was true: 'If you just work hard, put your mind to something, and go for it you can be successful, like the American dream.' This became real in all the ego trappings that were there—limousines, servants and people gloating over you.

It was in prison when I really came to know the Lord and His peace — real meaning, real identity, real purpose and real security. The statements of two men really influenced my thinking: Alexander Solzhenitsyn, the Russian professor and philosopher, said while in prison, 'Bless you, bless you prison for being in my life because it is there laying on the prison straw and rotting that I realized that the purpose of life is not pr osperity as we have been led to believe but the maturing of the soul'.

Blaise Pascal, the inventor of the computer, said, *There is a hole in our lives we try to fill with money, power, sex, drugs, work, recreation or any false idol that gets hold of our soul.*

The Grace Period

The three basic types of judgment are:

1) **Justice:** being convicted of a crime and receiving the full penalty you deserve;

2) **Mercy:** being given a lesser punishment for your offense;

3) **Grace:** someone else accepting the punishment for you.

In God's design, Jesus paid the price for us but we must accept His grace on our behalf if we want to receive His full blessing in our lives. The term *grace period* came from God's allowance of a reasonable time to accept Him or taking action for the atonement of our mistakes (missing the mark). For a long period of time, we may not see or sense the consequences of our wrong actions because of God's grace. Sometimes He's waiting and hoping for repentance.

So the grace period is time between our mistake and our day of accountability, here or before Him.

Getting Balance

Frank Brown is the former CEO of *Arthur Treacher's Seafood*, and the former President of *Shoney's, Captain D's* division. In these positions, in the fast moving and growing restaurant business, he traveled extensively and worked long hours. Leaving corporate life to become a franchisee himself in Utah was his next big challenge. Through his drive, energy, and hard work, his life was becoming unbalanced.

That spring, he and his wife and family attended their older son's college graduation in Tennessee and had a great time. After returning to Utah, Frank and his wife were awakened at 2:00 a.m. and told that their daughter and other son were in a car accident. He tearfully tells how he and his wife rushed back to Tennessee on a 7:00 a.m. flight only to find their son was okay, but their daughter was brain dead.

> *No Jesus,*
> *No Peace*
>
> *Know Jesus,*
> *Know Peace*

Having been raised in an Assemblies of God church, Frank never lost his faith in God. He recounts, *All things work together for good for those who love the Lord.*

Frank says today that experience was a turning point in his life. *It brought me back in focus on the important things in life. Today, I live a much more balanced life of God, family, and then work in the right priority.*

Today with all the pressure of a fast-growing public company, he teaches Sunday School to adults which helps him stay focused, grow spiritually, and serve others. He says, *As the teacher, I always learn more than the participants, but it is so rewarding when someone says, 'your teaching touched me and helped me change.'*

Being Carried

President Ronald Reagan, addressing the National Prayer Breakfast in Washington in 1982, offered these remarks:

> *Failure leads to success, if you learn from it.*
>
> **Chuck Coker**

Those of you who were here last year might remember that I shared a story by an unknown author, a story of a dream he had had. He had dreamt that he walked down the beach beside the Lord. And as they walked, above him in the sky was reflected each experience of his life. And then reaching the end of the beach,

195

he looked back and saw the two sets of footprints extending down the way, but suddenly noticed that every once in a while there was only one set of footprints. And each time, they were opposite a reflection in the sky of a time of great trial and suffering in his life. And he turned to the Lord in surprise and said, 'You promised that if I walked with You, You would always be by my side. Why did You desert me in my times of need?' And the Lord said, 'My beloved child, I wouldn't desert you when you needed Me. When you see only one set of footprints, it was then that I carried you.'

Well, when I told that story last year, I said I knew, having only been here in this position for a few weeks, that there would be many times for me in the days ahead when there would be only one set of footprints and I would need to be carried, and if I didn't believe that I would be, I wouldn't have the courage to do what I am doing.

Shortly thereafter, there came a moment when, without doubt, I was carried. (Later he referred to recovering from the bullet he took in the assassination attempt). *Well, God is with us. We need only to believe. The psalmist says, 'Weeping may endure for a night, but joy cometh in the morning.'*

Speaking for Nancy and myself, we thank you for your faith and for all your prayers on our behalf. And it is true that you can sense and feel that power.

I've always believed that we were, each of us, put here for a reason, that there is a plan, somehow a divine plan for all of us. I know now that whatever days are left to me belong to Him.

THE MORAL OF THE STORIES:

1. As we worship false idols of goals, activities or habits, we get entrapped in a *catch 22* which we struggle to break. Yet, struggles can be the things that God uses to fashion us for bigger and better things. Struggles can lead to *wake-up calls* which get our attention, get us refocused to seek Him. He allows our mistakes and failures to continually build our character.

2. If we won't listen and be humble, God will allow circumstances to convict us, bring us to maturity and get our attention.

3. During Old Testament times many people worshipped false gods as statues or idols. Today those false idols are more commonly termed *The Seven Sins of the Heart*. (Note: *What Do We Worship?* in Personal Study Guide in back of the book).

4. God loves each of us the same whether we are committed to Him or not. For example, Jim Bakker, the television evangelist of the 1980s, got caught in some of the same traps of pride, lust and greed as nonbelievers. He was trying to serve two gods, himself with his human addictions and the one true God. Having two masters never works. God is jealous and eventually we trip ourselves.

False Gods: Sins of the Heart

Problem: Our *spiritual vacuum* causes us to seek God; yet, misinformed and unaware, many of us get trapped into worshipping false idols instead.

Causes: Insecurities, deceit, fear, seeds of pain in the heart, bad habits, wrong role models and culture, and the sins of our parents cause us to miss God's guidance.

Outward Confirmations: Denial, defensiveness, blaming others, physical appearance, hiding the truth, wrong habits.

Healing Occurs Through: Admitting a problem, seeking or granting forgiveness, prayer (asking for help), immersion in the Word of God, counseling, fellowship, support groups, divine forgiveness, and love, love and more love. The greatest healing comes through a personal relationship with Christ and the spirit of God flowing through you.

5. Jamie Colter, the CEO of Lone Star Steakhouse and Restaurant, makes the statement, The *biggest predictor of future failure is your current success.* We can individually or corporately be riding an incredible wave of success. It seems that we can't make a mistake. Climbing the ladder of success or growth in economic terms seems to cover a lot of the barnacles that we gather as we go through life looking at the short term, or chasing what the world calls success. If the motives are wrong, failure or defeat will eventually catch up with us.

> *Success is 99% failure.*
> **Sacchiro Honda**
> **Founder of Honda**

6. Experience can be the best or the worst teacher. If your family, friends or even business have been learning the wrong principles, such as pride, egotism, lust, addictions, laziness, envy, anger and greed, they will face the consequences. There is only one true Master to serve, the one who created us. The world is full of deceit and false idols.

7. Many people relate to or find comfort in leaders, athletes, movie stars or media personalities. They can be good heroes if they know and respect the truth. Unfortunately, when these personalities are deceived and self-centered, they become bad examples. Many unknowledgeable or arrogant people find comfort in relating to their misdeeds, saying *If they can do it, it's okay, so can I.* Eventually they will pay the price.

> **Additional Wisdom**
> *Each man has his own prison.*
> **Johnny Cash**
> *The best doctors are former patients*
> *For some people things have to get worse before they get better.*

8. God's truths work whether we are atheist or devoted Christian. He loves each of us whether we know Him or not.

Movement To And From His Truths

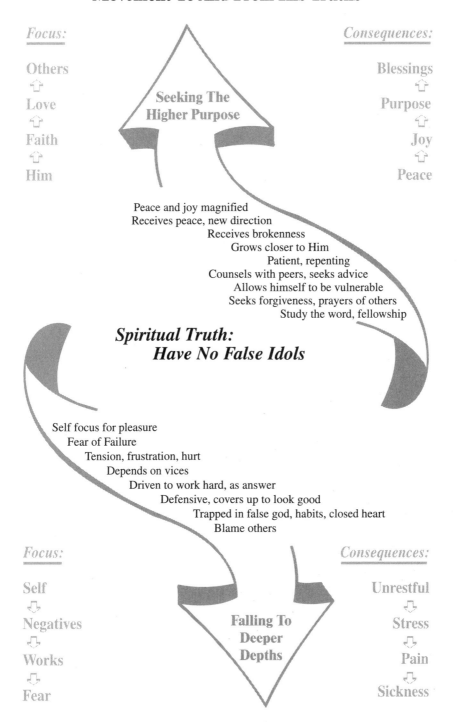

Focus:

Others
⇧
Love
⇧
Faith
⇧
Him

Seeking The
Higher Purpose

Consequences:

Blessings
⇧
Purpose
⇧
Joy
⇧
Peace

Peace and joy magnified
Receives peace, new direction
Receives brokenness
Grows closer to Him
Patient, repenting
Counsels with peers, seeks advice
Allows himself to be vulnerable
Seeks forgiveness, prayers of others
Study the word, fellowship

Spiritual Truth:
Have No False Idols

Self focus for pleasure
Fear of Failure
Tension, frustration, hurt
Depends on vices
Driven to work hard, as answer
Defensive, covers up to look good
Trapped in false god, habits, closed heart
Blame others

Focus:

Self
⇩
Negatives
⇩
Works
⇩
Fear

Falling To
Deeper
Depths

Consequences:

Unrestful
⇩
Stress
⇩
Pain
⇩
Sickness

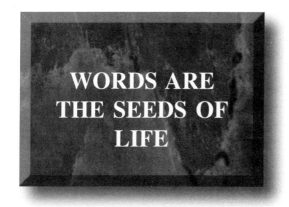

WORDS ARE THE SEEDS OF LIFE

Spiritual Truth: *Don't use God's name in vain.*

Character Quality: *Praise with your words.*

Words to the Heart

Sister Helen Mrosla isn't famous or world-renowned but her story is one that would touch anyone's heart. In her first year of teaching in Morris, Minnesota, her third grade class had a number of rowdy kids who seemed to continually pick on each other and make fun of one another. She became so frustrated that she decided to take positive action.

She took single sheets of notebook paper and wrote the name of each student at the top. As she passed around each paper she asked every student to write one positive thing about every other student on their paper as it went around the room. It took practically the whole afternoon but it seemed to change the tone of the class and set a proper atmosphere for the rest of the school year.

But that is only half the story. Ten years later one of the students from that class died in the Vietnam War. At his funeral, the young man's father stood up and showed everyone a worn and tattered piece of notebook paper. It had obviously been folded and refolded and had some old scotch tape holding it together where it had been torn. It was the list that the boy had been given by his classmates in the third grade. He had kept it all those years.

His Commanding Officer found it on my son's body after he died, the father said. *He kept it in his shirt pocket so that he could pull it out and read it whenever he was feeling blue.* Sister Helen, who repeated the story years later in *Reader's Digest,* noted that there were four other classmates from that particular class at the funeral. Three of them had kept their list all those years. Encouraging words can make a dramatic impact on the life of another person.

Words Hold Power

If you were asked the provocative question, *What is the most powerful instrument or influence in the world,* what would you say? God used His tongue to create the whole earth and used the words, *Let there be light,* to speak light and life into existence. As Dr. Robert Schuller says, *Because God, the Creator, designed the human being in His image, bearing His honored name, we are designed to become co-creators with Him. Words hold the power to creativity. Creative words generate energy; negative words drain out energy. A single word can turn you on, or it can turn you off. Negative words can diffuse your enthusiasm for a project. A positive word releases positive energy and becomes a creative force.*

Many men forget God all day and ask Him to remember them at night.

CHARACTER QUALITY

- Praise With Your Words -

Words are thoughts and containers filled with emotions, meanings, mental pictures, information and direction that are planted and grow in our hearts (spirit) and dictate our emotions. Scripture refers to the tongue and its words as a rudder on a ship; with the slightest turn it changes directions and moves the body, soul and spirit.

Don't use God's name in vain has a deeper meaning beyond merely refraining from profanity. Dr. Robert Schuller says, *The gift of words are to be used to communicate respect to the rest of the members of the human family to the end and for the purpose of creating mutual affirming and enriching relationships.*

When language is used to insult, ridicule, embarrass, demean, belittle or dishonor another member of the family, we put stress on ourselves and relationships. In the end God's name is the head of the family and the name of every other member of the human family are disgraced. Precious relationships are not enriched, rather they are deprived of dignity and left impoverished.

You can tell the depth of a man's or woman's character by the choice of their words—not by their length or vocabulary, but their respect, attitude and motives.

Very few of us realize that words are spiritual, as well as mental and physical in nature and control our interactions and relationships with God and our fellowman.

Early Values

Words shape our character and values. Especially in our early years, they get so deeply implanted in our hearts that they are hard to tear out or replace. Some examples:

- **Charles "Red" Scott**, the highly-respected executive who has built a diversified group of companies through acquisitions, grew up in the small town of Paris, Texas. His parents told him, *Always love your God, your family and your country. In honor, do what is right and have the courage to stand up for your beliefs, no matter what*.

- **Jim Moran**, the automobile giant raised in Chicago, said his mother taught him her values: *Be on time; keep your word; don't take what doesn't belong to you; and if you do something—do it right*.

- **Conrad Hilton**, hotel magnate raised near Santa Fe, New Mexico, said his mother taught him the value of prayer: *Take all your problems to God. He has the answers that we don't.*

- **J.C. Penney**, department store executive raised on a Missouri farm, heard his father say, *Love your neighbor as yourself, and never forsake the Golden Rule.*

- **Walter Anderson**, editor of *Parade* magazine, said his mother encouraged him to read and it became his ticket out of poverty. He regularily spent hours at the library.

- **Robert Crandall**, CEO of American Airlines, said, *My parents taught me the value of truth—you did what you said you would do; to follow the straight and narrow path and to do your best in everything. One day I stole a pumpkin and my father marched me by my ear to apologize to the man I stole it from.*

- **Rich DeVos**, co-founder of Amway, said his father was filled with the dream of starting his own business. It never happened for him, but his conversations with Rich had such an impact that it became his destiny to start a business, and to enthusiastically help others.

- **Dr. Ben Carson**, world-renowned doctor of neurosurgery, said his mother forced him to read two books a week, and to overcome the name-calling he got from other children. She said, *Learn to do your best, and God will do the rest.*

If the words from parents, teachers and friends are positive, and in line with God's truth, they carry us through life to be blessed and productive. But if parents or teachers tell a child, *You are worthless. You won't amount to anything.* or *I hate you.* Rather than, *I love you no matter what,* people struggle to overcome the impact of those negative words. Their emotional damage can curse a life, without the Truth of God.

WORDS

A careless word may kindle strife,
A cruel word may wreck a life,
A bitter word may hate instill,
A brutal word may smite and kill.
A gracious word may smooth the way,
A joyous word may light the day.
A timely word may lessen stress,
A loving word may heal and bless.

(*The War Cry*)

Words of Creativity

Have you ever been at a task force meeting in a corporation when somebody offered a particularly creative idea? There seems to be an excitement, enthusiasm and an energy flow because of the uniqueness of the idea. Then somebody says, *Look, guys, what you are proposing doesn't make any sense at all and won't work because we tried that three years ago.* Those words can deplete enthusiasm, destroy morale and create bitterness and jealousy, even though they may not have intended to do so. Energy is drained by the negative statement of one person. This helps each of us understand why in every brainstorming meeting the facilitator says, *There are no bad ideas, so save your criticism until I call for them.*

Words Affect Our Health

Doug Leatherdale, President and CEO of St. Paul Companies, reported that *The American Medical Association estimates that 80% or more of medical problems are stress related. The estimated cost is $50 billion annually*." Charles Mayo, who cofounded the Mayo Clinic, says, "*Worry affects circulation, heart, glands and the whole nervous system. I have never known a man who died from overwork, but a lot who died from doubt.*

Scripture says that words are seeds that are planted in our heart. Words express emotions and take root in our spirit or heart. It is the emotions of words that create joy, peace, doubt or worry in our life. Negative words create stress, and stress leads to sickness or ill health.

Dr. Ken Cooper, who coined the phrase, *Aerobics*, and author of many best sellers, says that there are two basic kinds of belief from the scientific point of view. The first is **extrinsic** belief, almost a rote or mechanical affirmation of convictions of spiritual faith. He says, *The distinguishing feature of this sort of belief is that it remains in the head and never makes it to the heart. Various studies prove that this type of belief does not improve a person's spiritual status, emotional well-being, or physical health.*

Give attention to My words; incline your ear to my sayings. Do not let them depart from your eyes; keep them in the midst of your heart; for they are life to those who find them, and health to all their flesh.

Proverbs 4:20-22

Intrinsic belief is characterized by a spiritual commitment to the meaning of life, heartfelt prayer and a quest to be changed. This kind of inner conviction — which may be accompanied by, but never limited to, outward, external observance is the key to real spiritual power.*" Real spiritual power is rooted in and created by the Word of God.

Decision Making

By God's design, seeds planted in fertile soil produce fruit: sometimes sweet (like flowers and strawberries), sometimes bitter or poisonous (like weeds and poison berries). The Bible says words are the seeds of our heart or spirit. Positive words are continuously filled with faith, meanings, solutions

> *Any fool can count the seeds in an apple. Only God can count the apples in one seed.*
>
> **Robert Schuller**

and willingness to take risks. Positive words are sweet and produce fruits of love, joy, contentment and peace. Bitter words produce hurt, depression, frustration or hate. The interpretation of words are the result of life's learning experiences, attitude, faith and inheritance.

Brian Tracey, internationally known author, trainer and consultant from San Diego, says, *100% of our decisions are based on our emotions*. Our emotions are controlled by our heart, and the positive or negative meaning inside us. As we make a decision it runs by our brain and heart simultaneously. The brain, which is the soul, may say *good idea* and the heart (spirit) says *watch out for hurt*. Unforgiven and unhealed hurts are slow to go away without God's influence.

We can't make a decision until the words we receive, and their meaning to us, are interpreted, judged and given a heart-felt response. It is impossible to be fully objective unless we can remove our emotions, which we cannot do.

Love or Perish

It is recognized by physicians and scholars that our heart or spirit is tied directly to the root of our sickness, diseases or peace. In the book, *None of These Diseases*, by S. I. McMillen, M.D. and Dr. E. Stern, M.D., the chapter on *Love or Perish* focuses on what he terms the psychosomatic illnesses. There are carnal attitudes and emotions which come from the seeds of negative words which we place in our heart and which get translated into stress or illness.

Dr. McMillen uses a list of corresponding diseases which cause emotions that he has extracted from a noted psychiatric textbook. Psychiatrist Smiley Blanton, says, *Without love, thoughtfulness and keen consideration of others — we become much more likely to perish from a variety of diseases of the body and mind.* He continued by quoting international psychiatrist, Alfred Adler, *The most important task imposed by religion has always been **love thy neighbor**...it is the individual who is not interested in his fellowman who has the greatest difficulties in life and provides the greatest injury to others. It is from such individuals that all human failings spring.* Dr. Adler based his conclusions on a careful analysis of thousands of patients. He held that *the lack of love is responsible for all human failures.*

When I quote the Bible, reports Dr. Adler, *to patients who are suffering physically and mentally from the lack of love, some of them retort that it is very difficult to change one's feeling — to change hate to love.* That is true. Psychologists support this view, for we, as humans, cannot gain complete control of our feelings. Yet, psychologists also state that our will can control our actions. *What we will to do is usually what we will do. Our will can give us freedom from bondage to our fickle emotions.*

Notice that there is one word which overcomes all the negative attitudes that produce disease. The word is **"Love"** with all its meanings. As you study this, you will soon realize **Love** is the most important word, seed, emotion and container. God created us in **Love**, protects and forgives us out of Love and sent His only son to die for us out of **Love**.

When Jesus was asked what was the greatest commandment of all, He said, ***Love** your Lord God with all your heart, soul and might, and **Love** your neighbor as yourself.* God loved us enough to create us and then send His only son. He invented **Love**. He is the only true source of **Love**. We must seek Him to receive His full measure in our lives and then we will start to radiate it to others.

The following chart compares the definition of Love from the Bible with corresponding disease-causing emotions directly from Dr. Kolb's textbook.

* LOVE	ATTITUDES THAT PRODUCE DISEASE
Is patient.	Frustration Discontent
Is kind.	Aggressiveness
Does not envy.	Envy Jealousy
Does not boast	Seeking attention
Is not proud	Over-valued body concept
Is not rude	Taking attitude
Is not self-seeking	Selfishness Greed
Is not easily angered	Anger Rage Irritability
Keeps no record of wrong	Resentment Hatred
Does not delight in evil	Death wishes for others Sexual fantasies
Rejoices with the truth	Dejection Desperation
Always protects	Competitiveness
Always trusts	Anxiety Doubt Striving for security Paranoia
Always hopes	Fear Despair Discouragement
Always perseveres	Irresponsibility Apathy

* Taken from I Corinthians 13:4

Heart of a Newborn

Your environment/culture are the values you learn or are exposed to – truth and deceit. Rain, shine – lightning (tragedy).

New fertile soil for good or evil seeds of emotions

Weeds inherited from father and mother

Fruit bearing trees with Love.

Heart of an Adult

Serious **trash** is buried here. When a flood of stress or frustration comes, the trash rises to the surface creating new problems.

Weeds represent words/emotions of pain, i.e., anger, envy, hate, jealousy, fear, greed...

The **forgiveness** valve to release the trash of our lives. We need to surrender them to our Lord and ask forgiveness of Him and those we have offended.

Words of Love bear fruit -- take root, i.e. kindness, patience, giving, humble, faith, hope...

Heart of a Spiritual Believer

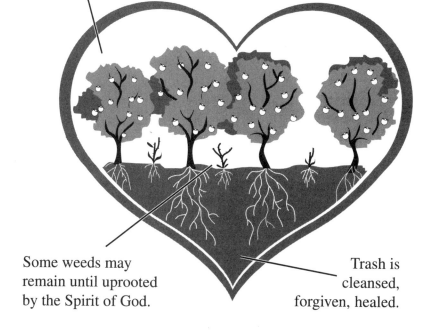

Some weeds may remain until uprooted by the Spirit of God.

Trash is cleansed, forgiven, healed.

The Word of God Heals and Nourishes

Fruit bearing seeds nurtured and growing can choke off weeds... the Bible is the source of love, truth and spiritual growth.

The amount of hurt or love in our heart controls our emotions, attitudes and decision making. Only the loving word of God can heal us of the hurt planted there.

Love produces sweet fruit of kindness, patience, forgiveness, joy, peace... to give unselfishly and receive back with humility.

211

Emotional Intelligence

Emotion

in Latin means:

"The Spirit that

moves us."

Dr. Robert Cooper, the champion of and noted author of the book, "Executive EQ" (Emotional Intelligence) explains his focus as the ability to understand and effectively apply the power and acumen of emotions as a source of information, energy, trust, creativity, and influence. He believes that more than 90 percent of trust and believability in our organizations is linked to Emotional Intelligence, not IQ.

Cooper says, "Our emotions contain our histories–every chapter and verse of every experience, deep understanding, and relationship in our lives." EQ is becoming known as an important management issue. More and more major employers recognize that the emotions an employee brings from life influences performance and productivity and that culture, communication, recognition, empathy, and praise is having enormous impact on their bottom line.

Emotions come from the depth of heart and are translated into words every day.

Faith and Health

Another recent study has linked good health with faith. The latest, done by Duke University, studied 4,000 North Carolinians age 65 or over. Results showed individuals in the sample group were 40 percent less likely to have high blood pressure when they participated in religious activities.

Their research shows that religious people are less depressed, have healthier immune systems, and deal better with addictions than the nonreligious.

Dr. Harold Koenig, who headed the study, respected in the International Journal of Psychiatry in Medicine that, "Older residents who attended religious services at least once a week had consistently lower diastolic readings, as did those who read the Bible or prayed regularly."

DISCRETION

The ability to use my words, actions, and attitudes toward the most **desirable consequences**

vs. simplemindedness

CHARACTER
TRAINING
INSTITUTE

THE MORAL OF THE STORIES:

1. The spirit and depth of His truth is that God used the seed of His words to create earth and life. Used against His truths, words harm. Used in harmony with His truths, there are words, thoughts and emotions that command and lead our lives in goodness.

2. Proverbs says, *As a man thinketh in his heart, so is he.* We think first with our heart and emotions, then with our brain.

3. The body is fed with food. The mind is fed with knowledge, communication and mental stimulation. The heart is fed with words and the emotions they represent.

4. There is only one source of words that heal, build, love, restore, and forgive. Those words are written by the Author of our creation in scripture. Without being humble, open and teachable before Him, they will never produce the full love he intended for each of us.

5. Words put our emotions on an upward or downward cycle in life. They command spiritual life and death. They allow the word of God to penetrate the heart

through study and fellowship and stabilize our emotions through His love.

6. Scripture words are more blessed than money. They buy peace, joy, fulfillment, and healing of the heart — eternal things that last forever. Words of hate do the opposite and cause harm, pain, and kill the human spirit. Unfortunately people who hold hate, bitterness, jealousy and envy in their hearts toward another person robs their heart of joy. These negative emotions hurt them far more inside than they hurt the person they hate. The demise of our human values is a result of our ignorance toward our Creator's design and it lessens opportunities to reach our hearts.

7. Words command body, soul and spiritual movements. Our choice of words is critical. This is where the Power of Positive Mental Thinking is derived.

8. While food, sleep and exercise are critical to the body's healing, most sickness can be traced to stress (created by the negative consequences of words, thoughts and actions). They manifest themselves in mental illness or physical stress on an organ or system of the body. It is like a balloon that has to burst from the stress of too much air. The peace of mind that only God can give overcomes stress.

9. Bullets, AIDS, and drugs can kill your body but not your spirit. However, words can kill the spirit or they can bring life.

10. If we seek peace of mind, without knowing Him, we may find temporary comfort in the words of a novel, movie or friend, attempting to fill the void. The deeper our emotional hurt and experiences they represent, the stronger the urge to seek out release in sex, violence, or revenge.

> *The line between good and evil runs through the heart of every individual.*
>
> **Alexander Solzhentsyn**

What Is An Attitude

It is the "advance man" of our true selves.

Its roots are inward but its fruit is outward.

It is our best friend or our worst enemy.

It is more honest and more consistent than our words.

It is an outward look based on past experiences.

It is a thing which draws people to us or repels them.

It is never content until it is expressed.

It is the librarian of our past.

It is the speaker of our present.

It is the prophet of our future.

Movement To And From His Truths

Focus:

Others
⇧
Love
⇧
Faith
⇧
Him

**Seeking The
Higher Purpose**

Consequences:

Blessings
⇧
Purpose
⇧
Joy
⇧
Peace

Honor God
Receive positive visions
Less stress in your life
Emotions stablize
Share His word with others
Praise God with others
Knowledge of power of words
Watching your tongue
Respect love for others
Respect for His name

*Spiritual Truth:
Don't Use God's
Name In Vain*

Attitudes "Everyone does it"
God's not listening
Words have no negative consequences
My words describe how I feel
Result significant lack of knowledge
Get back at other people
Frustration, personal offense, no forgiveness
Emotions are hurt deeper
Mental breakdown, depression

Focus:

Self
⇩
Negatives
⇩
Works
⇩
Fear

**Falling To
Deeper
Depths**

Consequences:

Unrestful
⇩
Stress
⇩
Pain
⇩
Sickness

THE PROBLEM WITH RELIGION

Spiritual Truth: *Keep the Sabbath Holy.*

Character Quality: *Rest and Listen in Him.*

Prayer is the Hub

In the 1920s, Conrad Hilton, the founder of the Hilton Hotel chain, struggled to raise a million dollars for his first major hotel in Dallas. So he developed the gift and talent to raise money, impress bankers, and "make the deal happen." He built a chain of twelve hotels before the Great Depression hit.

During the Depression, his business was starved for cash. He refused to declare bankruptcy, as so many recommended he do, because his good name and good credit rating were vital to his business. A supplier to whom he had once owed $100,000 (and faithfully paid each month) sued him for the final $178. But his employees believed in him. One employee surprised Conrad by giving him $300, his life savings, just to help the company.

As his ownership in the hotels eroded, he somehow miraculously avoided bankruptcy several times by carrying out his mother's advice: *Some men jump out of windows, some quit and some go to church. Pray, Connie, pray harder, and don't you dare give up.* Conrad went to church each morning before work for prayer.

Conrad believed that Prayer was the answer. *It is our means of communication with God. You can speak to Him anytime, night or day, and you can know with certainty that He is listening to you. . . there are no call letters. . . you are free to send any message you want. For me, personal living is fulfilling our place in the world, and the faithful use of our talents— each of these is a spoke in the circle of successful living. Prayer is the hub that holds the wheel together. Without our contact with God, we are nothing.*

Lead Us Father

Not everyone recognizes Grant Teaff, Executive Director of the American Football Coaches Association and former head coach of the Baylor University Football Team. In 1963 he was head coach of the McMurry College Indians, and they had just lost a game in Monroe, Louisiana. They had chartered a plane and were heading home with heads hung low in disappointment. Just after they had taken off, the pilot decided he was going to swing back and land. As he returned for the landing, the plane bounced back into the air again. One propeller and the landing gear were broken. The pilot came back to Grant and told him that they were going to Shreveport (SAC Base) and attempt to make a crash landing.

There was utter silence on the plane. The lights went off. Finally one of the boys turned to Grant and said, *Coach, will you lead us in prayer?* So he said in prayer as everyone held tightly to their seats, *God, You have a plan, purpose and will for our lives and if You will spare our lives we will do everything in our power to fulfill Your plan.* As he said that prayer, his own life flashed before

> **When you're green you're growing, when you're ripe you're rotten.**

him—his wife, his family and his relationship to God.

The plane crashed and caught fire but miraculously everyone escaped without harm. The anxious news media wanted the story but Grant simply told them that *God has got a plan for our lives*. The next day as the team assembled, one of the boys suggested that they form a club and vow to stay in

CHARACTER QUALITY

- *Rest and Listen in Him* -

To look like Mr. Universe or Miss America, in addition to good genes, you need the right balance of diet and exercise. We all recognize that it takes a certain discipline to gain the right figure or improve the look of the body. Yet if we would like to be as smart as Albert Einstein and weren't born with the same mental genius, then our next best alternative is to start reading, learning, listening and researching. We would be filling our brain with every fact, figure and bit of information that would help us accomplish our mental goals.

It is the same for a spiritual journey with God. This journey requires exercising our spirit through a relationship with Him pursuing personal growth, Sunday worship, reading the Bible, fellowshipping with others and seeking His direction.

This is the very principle that God is laying out for each of us with this truth. It is not about religion; it is about a personal relationship with Him. It is not about doing the right works but about growing in grace and faith.

Growth is one of the keys to life. It starts with the seed—the word of God that brings peace to the human heart.

contact so they could see what God would do with each of their individual lives.

Humorously, they called the club the "Brotherhood of Indian Belly Landing Experts." They ordered cards with the club name but the printer had to abbreviate the name. When they received the cards, they were pleasantly surprised that they were known as the BIBLE Club.

If you put money in savings it grows, if you put money in the offering plate you grow.

At the 20 year reunion, not one of the men had been divorced, and they are all serving God in some capacity.

Russian Faith

Dr. Robert Schuller shares the story of Walter Anderson, the editor of *Parade Magazine. Walter came from the poor side of New York City and as a child was abused by an angry father. Considering Walter's negative home and childhood, he had no interest in a heavenly father, churches, a religion, especially since he had his fill of his earthly father. On his own he had managed fine by himself; he had no need for a belief system.*

That all changed when he met God in, of all places, a Russian cathedral before the fall of the Iron Curtain, as an American tourist. This is how he related the incident:

About 25 miles south of Moscow is a little cathedral called the Church of the Trinity. It is a Russian Orthodox church. I visited this little cathedral and was struck by the rope that ran down the center of the church. On one side were people who viewed the cathedral as a museum. On the other side were people who were believers. I was with a monk named Longin.

I heard this beautiful hymn — it was magnificent. I couldn't recognize it, but it touched me. Being a typical American, I looked to see where the choir was. I couldn't figure it out. I couldn't believe this beautiful hymn. Finally I asked Longin, "Where is the choir?"

Longin replied, 'As the believers come in they pick up the sound of the hymn, and as they leave, they stop so there is always, here in Russia, a continuing hymn.'

> **God speaks to those who take time to listen.**

I thought about these people who profess their belief and stand for what they believe — in a society which ridiculed the notion of God, which discouraged religion in nearly every form.

Still they stand; they continue to believe, and I asked Longin, 'How did you come to be a priest, a monk? How did you even learn to do this?'

'When I was a child,' he said, 'we were taught the stories of the Bible as legends.

All of the students read them as legends and myths. Then there came a moment when I read the stories differently; I believed them; I heard them differently from the other children.'

When Longin said that it came to me that I now heard the stories differently, and I too believed.

Vaccinated Christians

In a country like ours founded by men with a deep Christian belief, many Americans have been brought up in or attended church. Since spirituality is not physical and visible, it is not real to many who are "too intelligent" to believe in God. Society doesn't seem to emphasize God at work or at play. People know the story of Christ and see Him as a nice historical figure. Surveys confirm that 90% of Americans believe in God and many say *I'm a good person, isn't that enough?* They might say, *I live by the Ten Commandments - I've never killed anyone, committed adultery and don't steal.* Others see Christians as hypocritical, acting one way in church but another way during the week. Others are turned off by the words, *King* and *Lord.* After all those are medieval terms for oppressors who controlled the peasants. In truth, it means leader. Some say Christianity is boring, anti-fun and can't compete with the

Sunday morning entertainment found on television, movies, football or even golf.

Let it be known by all, that all types of believers and nonbelievers fall short of His plan and purposes. The word "sin" comes from the archers of medieval times when an archer *missed the mark*. Even the best Christian has *missed the mark* and unfortunately, given that we live in a world full of evil, we are all hypocrites at times, and will sin again. Yet, we can be forgiven through Christ. Religion is not the answer, it is a man-made system, with human faults. The answer is a personal relationship with God through Jesus Christ.

The Luck of the Irish

In 433 AD, St. Patrick brought Christianity to Ireland. To better help the Irish people to understand and remember the Trinity, he used the shamrock (three-leaf clover) to describe the Father, Son and Holy Spirit. It became so popular that it has become the national symbol of Ireland, and the symbol of good luck.

Amazing Grace

Ken Blanchard, co-author of *The One-Minute Manager* shares how he and his wife made a significant mistake in their early career by being church drop-outs. Ken was teaching at Ohio University and the pastor of their church, whom they really appreciated, was fired. He had become involved in student protests over the Vietnam war. He shares that, *Anger and disillusionment came crashing in on us. We thought 'If that's what church is all about, forget it.' We dropped out. Like so many people, we went to church only at Christmas and Easter for fifteen years.*

Years later, Ken sought a desire to know more about God sensing a need for a greater purpose and peace. The tremendous success of his books and company were not providing a sense of fulfillment. He talked with his good friend Bob Buford, a successful CEO and also an author. Ken could not see himself as a sinner. Bob explained it this way, *Ken, do you see yourself as good as God?* Ken said, *No, God is perfect.* Bob continued *Okay. On a scale of 1 to 100, let's give God 100. We'll give Mother Teresa 90 and a murderer 5. Ken, you are a decent sort and trying to help others. I'll give you 75. Now the special thing about Christianity is that God sent Jesus to make up the difference between you and 100. That's what grace is all about. It is not about deeds. If you accept Jesus as your Savior, no matter what your past has been, He rids you of your sins and brings you closer to 100.*

Ken realized that he had wrongfully viewed God in a religious context, thinking that doing good by achievement would bring him fulfillment and even get him into Heaven. Now, he often asks people in his management seminars these questions:

- How many of you have children?
- How many love those children?
- How many love your children depending upon their achievement?

Everyone admits that he or she would love their children whether they are high achievers or not. That's the way God is as well. He offers unconditional love.

Ken offers this view *If we can begin to accept unconditional love from our Father, we set the stage for acknowledging grace. Your focus no longer has to be out there with results, accumulation, power, acceptance, control, or earthly things. Now you can focus on your own sense of personal excellence and the journey – how to live your life. You can begin to live according to God's law.*

> *In Calcutta, people are starving physically. In America, people are starving emotionally. What people are hungering for is Love, that only God can provide.*
>
> **Mother Teresa**

225

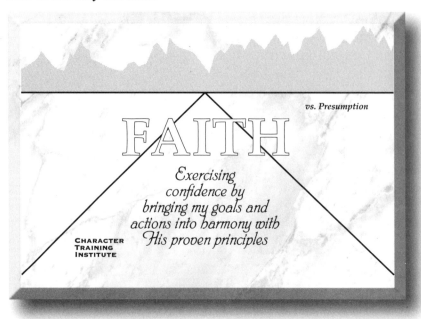

Religion is the Law Created by Man

Nowhere in the Bible does it say that God asks us to create churches with different denominations and doctrines. Pete Maravich said, *Religion sends more people to hell — denominations, religions and false religions. Christianity is the truth. Christianity is not a 100-yard dash, it is a marathon and just keeps going on and on.* Because of men's different levels of understandings, style, personality, personal growth, training and visions, different denominations have been created. Each Christian is on a personal journey, a walk with God, and He leads us through our different stages of growth, depending on our openness and commitment. Because of these denominational differences, Christians may appear hypocritical to the uninformed or non-believer. Nevertheless, the Bible is the common foundation and source for our Christian faith.

Dr. Ken Cooper talks about *extrinsic belief* and we see this type of belief in Northern Ireland (where Protestants battle Catholics), in Bosnia and the former Yugoslavian Republics, and in the Middle East, only to name a few. Those countries are being torn apart by religious strife. America has been blessed by God and our founders were blessed in that we have avoided internal religious wars. Most of us have been taught The Ten Commandments and to respect and honor freedom of religion and denominations. The American spiritual battle is not between different religions or denominations; it is for the heart (between truth and deceit, good and bad, jealousy, greed, and revenge, to name a few). The Great Crusades of Europe choked off many real spiritual opportunities to penetrate the hearts of European believers, and has caused them to become extrinsic rather than intrinsic believers.

Yet one of the most respected woman in the world, Mother Teresa, is from European Yugoslavia. She honored and served God, and is a shining example to the world of giving her best to honor Him. Others need to follow her example.

Lack of Spiritual Growth Can Produce:

- Emptiness
- Frustrations and tension
- Deep hunger for something unknown
- Great desire to be loved
- Economic stress
- Money with no joy or peace
- Failure, lack of success
- Physical pain, sickness
- Accidents
- Loss of job, loved one

Four Types of Believers

Generally, there are four different stages, or levels of belief, which categorize and explain where people are in relationship to the Christian faith:

1. **Non-believer** — Was often raised in the home where there is no basis for moral values, attitudes focus on entitlement, or *take what you can get.* Family love is absent, and very little respect for authority is practiced. God is not important *if* He even exists.

2. **Self-believer** — To be successful you have got to do *it*

227

your way, work hard within the system but use it for your own personal gain. If you can't see God, He must not be real, or care about you. The self-made goal is to seek your own personal satisfaction and "look out for number one."

3. **Moral believer** — Concerned about others, as well as self, and believes in God, particularly as a last resort. Attends church and believes in moral values. The goal is to be a good person, successful, and a contributor to society. If asked by the boss, though, he or she will go along with breaking some ethics or policies. Sees God by the size and shape of his own level of faith.

4. **Spiritual believer** — Seeks God's love, direction and will through a personal commitment. Sees his or her life as a spiritual journey, driven by God's values. Openly seeks and learns through the Bible, sharing with other Christians, through prayer and fellowship. As he or she sees God working in his life, God gets the credit. Understands the true meaning of love because the flow of God's love works through his life. He or she is God-centered and people-centered.

All four of these types of people have a little overlap, as we are always learning, growing, changing, and hopefully moving closer toward the spiritual Christian that God is calling all of us to become.

> *Don't be just a teacher, be a student teacher.*

The Spiritual Christian, as he or she grows and sincerely comprehends God's purpose for life, has more vision, joy and sense of fulfillment, and is not so concerned about material things.

Beyond Church

Tom Landry, the Hall of Fame football coach of the Dallas Cowboys, and Bernhard Langer, two-time winner of the Masters Golf Tournament, have something in common. One was raised a Protestant and the other a Catholic, and both attended church every Sunday. Their common thread is that a friend invited them to a Bible Study. They each believed attending church made them a Christian. After all, they believed in God.

Later, they both confessed that attending that Bible Study opened their eyes, ears and hearts to a whole new journey and commitment to the Lord. Meeting Him personally brought joy, peace and understanding they had never known before, especially in their stressful athletic careers with the

> *Some people complain because God put thorns on the roses, while others praise Him for putting roses among thorns.*

pressure they had both faced. They understood the old adage that "parking yourself in a garage does not make you a car," any more than attending church makes you a Christian. It takes faith and commitment to expand our journey in life.

Why Go to Church?

Bill McCombes, President of Infoquest, says *It's just a matter of perspective and how much you want to experience. For example, if someone asks you what happened with your favorite team, you have 5 ways to know:*

    a. Hear the score

    b. Read about it in the paper

    c. Watch it on TV

    d. Sit in the stadium; or

    e. Playing, taking action in the event, being part of the team.

Obviously, church is best when we are a participant and we grow by the experience.

Sharing Faith

The greatest decision I ever made as a coach, says Florida State Coach Bobby Bowden, *was instituting a daily devotional with our coaches and staff. We meet for staff meetings every morning and take five minutes before we get started and a different member shares a Biblical truth or motivating statement that will help each one of us grow personally.*

Every Friday night before a game there is a team dinner and Bobby shares Scripture or a personal message about his walk with the Lord. He reminds the players that life after football is a real challenge and that each of us needs a "rock" to be anchored to. While Bowden has had a number of players drafted in the NFL, he reminds them that the average stay is only four years.

Tom Osborne and his staff at Nebraska and hundreds of other coaches around the country are involved in FCA (Fellowship of Christian Athletes, headquartered in Kansas City) and share their stories and help young men and women from high school to professionals become prepared for a life that is eternal.

The greatness of a leader is in his humility before God, not his eloquence before man.

Walk Their Talk

Truett Cathy, the founder of Chick-Fil-A, has personally been involved in leading a Sunday School class in his church for over 40 years. He has built a large camp for boys and girls and personally sponsors 45 foster children in five different homes. He also provides up to $10,000 in college scholarships for kids that work in his business.

Bo Pilgrim, Founder of the Pilgrim Pride Company (a $1 billion chicken processing business) has taught Sunday School for 24 years and has built a prayer tower open to the public in his home town of Pittsburg, Texas. He also provides 45 different chaplains through the Marketplace Ministries organization of Dallas, Texas, to his 6,000 employees in four different plants.

Gil Stricklin, former staff member of the Billy Graham organization, is founder of this group that trains and supplies over 275 part-time pastors to companies in the Southeast and Northeast.(Note chapter 9).

Returning Your Call

Did you ever have a friend who only calls when he or she needs something, yet never offers to return the favor, or seem appreciative? Even if you have a heart to want to help, this can be annoying. You may stop returning their calls.

> *God blesses people and businesses who honor Him.*

Well, our Creator has the same nature. We were created in His image. That is why He wants a personal relationship. Yes, He will respond to an emergency or "House Call" in answering our prayers, but at the same time, that may be why He doesn't return our calls or answer our prayers. He is tired of being our "genie" — the magic lamp we use when we want something big.

We appreciate those most whom we can give to and who give back. God is no different and that is one of the reasons He seeks a personal relationship to go beyond the need to be the god of emergencies and become the God of a daily walk together. He desires to give and take in love and kindness, in little requests as well as large ones.

Is it any wonder why so many "good" people may not make it to Heaven?

THE MORAL OF THE STORIES:

1. The Lord is *not* calling us to put our faith in a religion or denomination, but to a personal relationship with Him.

2. Keeping the Sabbath holy is about drawing us closer to Him with a restful and open heart. Set aside quiet time to praise, pray, reflect and grow closer to Him.

3. Each of the first four commandments of The Ten Commandments is about having a personal relationship and walk with Christ. Churches or organizations which fail to teach these principles are missing the fulfillment of God's spiritual truths.

4. The Bible speaks to the spirit of man, we must be *born of the spirit* for the Word to become personally meaningful and reveal His truth.

5. All of us *miss the mark* (sin) and fall short of His righteousness in our lives, but through the urging of the Holy Spirit we will continue to grow more like Him.

6. The Bible says *My people perish from a lack of knowledge.* We must take the time to read His word, to find truth for the direction and purpose of our lives.

7. Moses brought the Truths of God, The Ten Commandments, down from the mountain top to the Jewish people who sought the *truths for success* in their new-found freedom. Jesus brought the *Spirit of the Truth* with a further explanation and understanding of the how, why and where of God's commands. His death was a sacrifice for our sins and our inability to measure up to His righteousness. But the journey continues as we grow closer to Him.

Five Ways He Talks To Us

1. The Holy Spirit touches our heart—through a soft inner voice or a real peace and calm from reading His Word. We gain wisdom, understanding, direction and insight as a result.

2. Through a friend, boss, spouse, employee or associate who gives us advice (often a confirmation or realization of His truth or direction for ourselves).

3. Warning signs—early indicator is a lack of peace of mind about trouble ahead.

4. Wake-up calls—profound problems or frustrations which occur because we are "missing the mark" or misguided. He is waiting for us to turn back to His truths.

5. Failures or tragedies that ultimately seem to mature us and bring us back to Him in a humble way.

God protects moral people for a *grace period* of time but will allow us to suffer the consequences of our negative actions. It is always a learning experience for us. Many of the experiences are humbling. If we don't humble ourselves before God and seek Him, He will allow us to become humble through the consequences of our actions.

Movement To And From His Truths

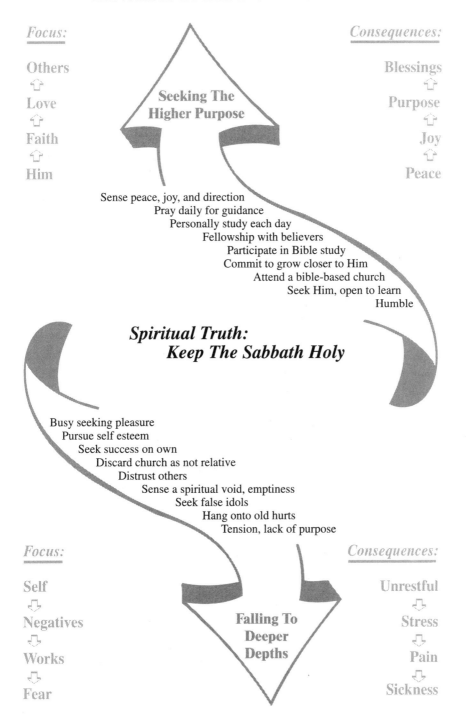

Focus:

Others
⇧
Love
⇧
Faith
⇧
Him

Consequences:

Blessings
⇧
Purpose
⇧
Joy
⇧
Peace

Seeking The Higher Purpose

Sense peace, joy, and direction
Pray daily for guidance
Personally study each day
Fellowship with believers
Participate in Bible study
Commit to grow closer to Him
Attend a bible-based church
Seek Him, open to learn
Humble

Spiritual Truth:
Keep The Sabbath Holy

Busy seeking pleasure
Pursue self esteem
Seek success on own
Discard church as not relative
Distrust others
Sense a spiritual void, emptiness
Seek false idols
Hang onto old hurts
Tension, lack of purpose

Focus:

Self
⇩
Negatives
⇩
Works
⇩
Fear

Consequences:

Unrestful
⇩
Stress
⇩
Pain
⇩
Sickness

Falling To Deeper Depths

THE BOTTOM LINE

Self-Centered or God-Centered?

In the 1980s, the J.C. Penney Company had to make some critical decisions about future strategies for business. David F. Miller was President of J.C. Penney Stores and Catalogue, and the decisions he and his team made set the company on a new course of growth and prosperity during a difficult retail era and the even more competitive decades ahead. Having had the privilege of knowing Jim Penney personally, Miller became a lay speaker sharing Jim Penney's story with his church members a few years ago. He recounts this story:

I would like to refer to this experience as Pastor's Appreciation Sunday. After listening to me, you will appreciate your pastor a lot more! On a serious note, each of us — in our lack of spiritual consciousness — gives ourselves credit for what we term our "success" in life. Frank Sinatra's popular song, 'I Did It My Way' has been a top hit for nearly two decades. Advertising slogans like 'You owe it to yourself' are seen and heard everyday. We generally believe it.

Positioned against this view is the consistent admonishment from both the Old and New Testaments to seek first the kingdom of God and His righteousness — to pursue a spiritual consciousness. Thus we live our lives with an eternal struggle: Should our focus be God-centered or self-centered? Self-focus most often proves to be destructive. Experiences from the life of Mr. James Cash Penney can help us better understand how dangerous and defeating such thoughts can be.

Jim Penney spent his youth in the small farming town of Hamilton, Missouri. His father — whom he credits for his understanding of ethical business behavior — was a circuit-riding preacher during the latter half of the 19th century. He served the church without pay while providing for his family by farming. Their existence was austere, even harsh — devoid of any material excesses. Mr. Penney, however, recalls those days in his writings with great warmth and certainly deep respect.

Commerce seemed to come naturally to Jim, and at the age of 8 he began raising pigs as a source of income to help his family. He was resourceful and energetic — and the pig population grew rapidly. Unfortunately, as he writes, 'I was doomed to disappointment. The pig-pen is an unpleasant neighbor during the hot summer months — a fact that was brought to my attention by complaints received by my father.'

Jim's father made him sell the pigs, telling him that he should respect the rights of his neighbors and not profit at someone else's expense. The senior Mr. Penney quoted 'The Golden Rule' to young Jim as the basis for his decision. Jim respected his parents, and adopted their beliefs as he began a merchant career in the local dry goods store as a combination stock boy/junior clerk.

His hard work and dedication eventually led to other opportunities, specifically in Colorado. His effort there resulted in the opening of his own store in financial partnership with his two former employers. An unlikely spot was selected — the small mining town of Kemmerer, Wyoming. The store was opened in April of 1902 — thus, the beginning of the J.C. Penney Company.

Borrowing from his parents' teachings — and through his own talents and hard work — he was immediately successful. While he required the same hard work and cooperation from those who joined him in his dream of building a retail empire, he was quick to recognize the value of sharing — not only the financial rewards — but in giving those who worked with him the opportunity to become partners, just as his former employer had given him.

He used the term, 'Associate,' rather than 'employee,' and profit sharing became one of the fundamentals in the early growth of the business. He looked for and accepted as partners only those who shared his ideals and willingness to sacrifice. In short, Mr. Penney may have been the first practitioner of what we refer to today as a "real business partnership" — dedication, hard work, loyalty and singleness of purpose on the part of the worker, reciprocated by recognition, sharing, financial reward, and a high degree of security on the part of the employer.

Perhaps most importantly, in guiding the business, he insisted on ethical dealings. In fact, in the beginning his stores were known as 'The Golden Rule Stores.' So he prospered. By 1917, just 15 years after the opening of that first store in Kemmerer, Wyoming — the Penney Company was financially sound...a rapidly expanding chain of 175 stores.

In keeping with this extreme confidence in his partners, Mr. Penney turned over the daily operations of the organization to a hand-picked, personally trained successor, Mr. Earl Sams. With Mr. Sams at the helm, Mr. Penney was free from day-to-day operations of the business.

He was in great demand as a speaker on his favorite subject — 'Christian Principles of Business.' He and his family traveled extensively, both at home and abroad. He was received worldwide by national leaders as a giant in retailing — an entrepreneur of enormous prestige. He co-founded Foremost Dairies to bring quality dairy products to the market at very competitive prices. You might say he was the original 'off-price" retailer.'

> **What lies behind us and what lies before us are tiny matters compared to what lies within us.**
>
> **Ralph Waldo Emerson**

Like many other men of wealth during this period, he saw Florida as a promise of the future. Using some of his accumulated wealth, he purchased tens of thousands of acres of Central Florida farm land, with the idea of shipping produce to the big eastern cities. His dream was to relocate families to Florida, where they would train and become partners in farming. He would bring quality, fresh produce to millions — just as he had done with clothing, dry goods, and dairy products.

Grateful for the sacrifices of his parents, he built and dedicated in their memory a retirement community for ministers

---

Why is The J.C. Penney Company Still In Business?

After 90 years, is it because:
- — they have good people and good products?
- — they have good strategy and culture?
- — they are flexible and adapt to change?
- — because God promises generations of blessings to a faithful founder?
- — or all of the above?

---

of all denominations. Even today, the town of Penney Farms in Northern Florida is regarded as a model community, boasting one of the highest educational levels of any city in the United States.

Expanding his interest in Florida, he became a central figure in one of the largest land booms in American history. He accepted the position of Chairman of the board of City National Bank of Miami to lend his name to the enterprise, although he had no intentions of managing the daily affairs of the bank. So, as the 20s drew to a close, Jim Penney would smile with satisfaction. He seemed to have conquered the world, although he clearly had not overcome the world. He had 'done it his way.' Then came "Black Tuesday."

The week of October 26, 1929, the New York Stock Exchange lost 21% of its value that week. Over the next thirty months, the paper wealth of those who had invested in America's financial empire plummeted by 81%. The land boom in Florida took the most severe hit of all. City National Bank of Miami was closed

— bankrupt. Mr. Penney's losses were heavy, but they represented a reasonably small portion of his total wealth.

His enormous holdings in the J.C. Penney Company, for the most part, were still intact. The company was being soundly managed by Mr. Sams and his partners. In fact, the chain was growing by absorbing other retailers as the depression took its toll.

Mr. Penney's name — and somehow his reputation — were inexorably intertwined with the bank in Miami. Thousands of depositors had lost their entire savings, trusting in the bank whose principle director was James Cash Penney. His name was often associated with the disaster in the headlines of the local papers. They asked — 'How could it happen? When so many had lost all, how could Jim Penney still remain secure and — by any standard — extremely wealthy?'

Those headlines devastated Mr. Penney. Unable to satisfy himself with a legal interpretation of his innocence, he borrowed millions against his Penney stock to keep the bank open — and also to continue supporting the J.C. Penney Foundation and his other philanthropic interests. As the stock market plummeted, he began to sell his Penney stock at now substantially reduced prices to cover these loans. The downward spiral continued, and in the end this once extremely rich man found his wealth totally depleted.

By 1931, the financial battle was over and James Cash Penney had lost. He was financially and emotionally broke — from king to pauper in just a few years. Where had he gone wrong? What had he done to deserve this devastation? He searched in vain for answers, but they would not come. He sank even lower, and a physician friend — unable to help — finally recommended his sanitarium in Battle Creek, Michigan for rest and treatment.

One night, while there, he became convinced that he would never see another day. He wrote a letter to his wife and children, asking for their forgiveness and understanding. After 57 years, he was certain he would depart this world in total defeat. He spent that night in tortured anguish, expecting to die, yet searching for some evidence — some sign — from his Creator that his life contained meaning.

Finally, the dawn came. He had survived the night, but only to face another dreaded day. In a weakened stupor, he wandered down the hall of the sanitarium — totally devoid of any self-confidence or pride of personal success. He was a lost soul in every respect. It was in this wretched, defeated condition that Mr. Penney began to find lasting answers to his life. Let me relate how he later described the experience:

"I passed a parlor in the sanitarium and heard a choir singing, 'God will take care of you.' A few people had gathered in the religious meeting and I felt urged to enter. In great weariness of spirit, I listened to the hymns, to the scripture reading, and to the prayers. Then, a profound sense of inner release came over me. A heavy weight seemed to be lifted from my spirit. I was amazed at my change, and in the days that followed, I regained mental and bodily health. Perhaps the feeling of death that night was a symptom of a new beginning born in me."

In that small religious meeting, Mr. Penney recognized

- *that being honest and moral were not enough, God wanted his mind as well, 'as a man thinketh, so is He.'*

- *that he must first seek the kingdom of heaven, and that all things would be added thereto.*

- *that he had lost nothing of value, that he was a child of God.*

- *that wealth and power, not God — had been the motivating factors in his life.*

- *that J.C. Penney Company was not the product of James Cash Penney, but the infinite mind of God working through His child, Jim Penney.*

Mr. Penney left that institution a few days later, having rearranged his personal priorities. "Blessed are the poor in spirit, for theirs is the kingdom of God." How divine these words of the first beatitudes must have seemed to Jim Penney.

He had finally realized that it was the divine consciousness within him that must be in charge of this life — the positive force that is available to all of us if we take the quiet time to listen. He vowed that what remained of his life would be given entirely to God. And so it was, for nearly 40 years, he used his influence, his skills, and his service in the application of Christian principles. He advised others to do the same, saying, those who have the greater part of their adult life before them should study with great earnestness the relation between Christ's two commandments — 'to love God and to love they neighbor as thyself.'

At James Cash Penney's death, Dr. Norman Vincent Peale's eulogy said of him, "He became ever more humble, with a disarming wonderment about him that these great things could happen to him. His benefactions and good work shall ever bless his name." That was high praise for a man who forty years earlier faced a life of total defeat. From that night in Battle Creek, Jim Penney had a never ceasing commitment to follow the first commandment: 'Love thy God with all thy heart, and with all thy soul and with all thy might.'

His story is a lesson for all of us who are tempted to focus on ourselves as the power behind our accomplishments and our success. 'Whosoever shall exalt himself shall be abased; and he that shall humble himself shall be exalted.'(Matthew 23:12).

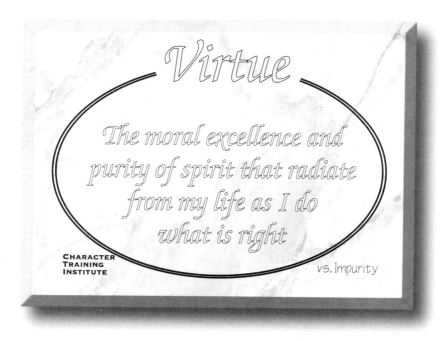

Virtue

The moral excellence and purity of spirit that radiate from my life as I do what is right

CHARACTER
TRAINING
INSTITUTE

vs. Impurity

My Way
(By Paul Anka, C. Francois, J. Revaux & G. Thibault)

And now the end is near, and so I face the final curtain.
My friend. I'll say it clear, I'll state my case, of which I am
    certain.
I've lived a life that's full,
I've tracked each and every highway, and much more
    than this,
I did it my way.

I have loved, I've laughed and cried, had my fill and my
    share of losing,
And now as tears subside, I find it all so amusing,
To think I did all that, not in a shy way,
I did it my way.

For what is a man, what has he got,
If not himself, then he has not,
To say the things he truly feels,
And not the words of one who kneels.

Let the record show,
I took the blows, and did it my way.

*Many people believe that "My Way," excerpted above,
is man's egotistical and prideful way of being in control.
Free will does give man the choice to "do it his way" or to
follow God, but only following God will lead to true peace,
joy and fulfillment, the spiritual wealth of life.*

THE MORAL OF THE STORY:

1. God's truths are calling us to three principles of:

    A. Character—*taking personal initiative*

    B. Spiritual—*personal relationship with Him*

    C. Moral —*loving our fellowman*

    J. C. Penney grasped and implemented the character and
    moral truths. He thought he had all that God had planned
    for his life. Through humility, he discovered what he had
    not understood...God wanted a personal relationship, to

love and be loved by Him. He wants the same from each of us. This is the secret to true wealth in life.

2. Any manufacturer has limitations on the use of their product, e.g., an automobile may not be designed for the desert or towing a boat, or a suit is designed for summer wear rather than winter. All products have limits to their use, stamina and longevity.

> *God is the manufacturer (designer and Creator) of each of our lives.*

Our limitations are listed in the "owner's manual," the Bible. The more improper use or stress we place on our body, soul and spirit, the greater the chance for pain or breakdown of the parts. He doesn't have to "raise a finger" when we get out of our lane. We eventually feel the pain of our consequences. He can wait for us to call Him (yet, He is there every moment ready to help).

3. Using our character talents and implementing the moral truths will lead us to achieve a higher level of success in business, career, relationships with family and others. It is the foundation for satisfying the customer and serving employees. Unfortunately, these truths are very hard to completely live by because of the deceit and pressure placed on us in the world. That is why we need to live by His spiritual principles first.

4. Many of us would say, *I believe in God and even call on Him when I really need Him. I'm a good person, Isn't that enough?* But I believe God is saying, *No, that is not enough. I have blessed you in many ways and want to love you more through a personal and spiritual relationship. I have greater plans for your life than being just a moral person.* Two out of three is not good enough.

5. God says, *Don't worship the wrong things. There is an eternity beyond this world that I have placed you in and I want the joy of leading you to a higher purpose and more fulfilling life here and beyond.*

> *Our conduct and His grace are more important than our accomplishments.*

> **God honors most those who honor Him and His ways.**

To come to Me, I need you to be humble like a little child, seeking My face and My word and I will reveal a new life to you forever and ever.

6. All righteous dreams or visions for businesses, careers, missions are inspired by the spirit of God. The closer we come to know Him, the more easily we will recognize and understand them. God will anoint people to accomplish His righteous purposes.

7. Every time we follow the Lord's command, we please Him and something happens which blesses us. When we disobey His truths, something negative happens – maybe not immediately (as if we are given a *grace period*), but eventually something happens. Why? Because we are spiritual people first. God doesn't have to raise a hand—it's the system He designed. His eternal truths, commands, and laws work in our lives by design. If we just follow the first and second commandments, *Have no other God before me or false idols,* our hearts will begin to change. That change will lead us to be receptive to all other truths.

– *Availability* –
vs. Self-centerdness

			1	2	3	4
			Making my own schedule			
5	6	7	8	9	10	11
and priorities SECONDARY to the wishes						
12	13	14	15	16	17	18
of those I serve						
19	20	21	22	23	24	25
26	27	28	29	30	31	CHARACTER TRAINING INSTITUTE

Summary of Truth

1. God loves us whether we know Him or never serve him.
2. As we live by His Truths, whether we know them or not, we grow and He blesses us.
3. He brought grace through the sacrifice of His Son, Jesus, most often covering us from evil through prayers, beliefs, and our actions.
4. Truth applies and works through individuals, families, organizations, and nations.
5. Americans are more prosperous and blessed because of the truths our founders set in motion. It is our culture, and we are reaping the harvest of that trust.
6. Economic prosperity is a result of using His Character Truths (gifts, talent, work, leadership) and Moral Truths (loving our neighbors—customers, employees, etc.)
7. True wealth comes from living by His Spiritual Truths (loving God in a personal relationship) and growing from the inside out in faith, peace, joy, and fulfillment—having little to do with money, possessions, or fame.
8. He is preparing us to live in Eternity (heaven) drawn to righteousness; as we mature and take on His image, nature, and character.
9. Through the decision man made in the Garden of Eden to be self dependent, God allows emptiness, frustrations, pain, adversity, and even death to humble us and be our teacher. He is waiting for us to surrender to Him for fullness of life.
10. His timetable is eternal, long–term and working to accomplish His plan.
11. Physical death is never final but God does not guarantee us heaven by just being a "good person."
12. The keys to our living are the word seeds of good or evil we plant in our heart.
13. The Bible is the word of God and nourishes the soul and spirit of our lives when we sincerely trust Him.
14. We are designed to live a God-centered life in the light of openness, honesty, trust, and loving relationships. The self-centered life is more easily trapped in deceit and wrong motives and expectations.

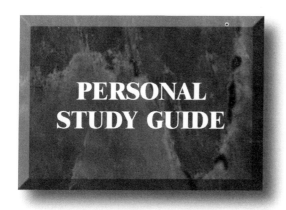

I. What Do We Worship?

As long as man and woman have existed on earth we have sought idols or gods to worship, to fill their own spiritual vacuum. In psychological terms, humans need to find a source of security—a place to rest, feel comfort, and call home; a place to hide from the unknowns of life, and be fulfilled, providing us with a rock and anchor. We seek those places from which to draw meaning and purpose, to find identity, to overcome our fears and doubts about the unknown and the things we don't understand and need to make sense of, for peace of mind. Humans long to find something to fill the vacuum that God placed in each of us, a vacuum that can only be filled by Him.

In the days of the Old Testament man created statues and golden calves; others worshipped the sun, the wind or the earth and called them gods. In American society, which is based on Christian Biblical principles, we have experienced the greatest prosperity in the shortest period of time of any nation on

> *I have learned that life is made up of lefts and rights, you need to take the right fork in the road.*
>
> **Terrell Davis**
> **1997 Super Bowl MVP**

earth. Yet so many of us are easily deceived, are ignorant or have become too "intelligent" to fall for a story of a savior dying on a cross. Being "saved" from what? Don't we already have the good life?

Most of us have chosen a variety of *false idols* to worship, to fill the inner need we experience. The Bible refers to them in different passages, and they are most often recognized as the *Seven Sins of the Heart.* Here are the examples below:

FALSE IDOLS

Problem: Our *spiritual vacuum* causes us to seek false idols which we become trapped into worshipping.

Causes: Insecurities, deceit, fear, seeds of pain in the heart, bad habits, wrong role model in the culture, or sins of parents.

Outward Confirmations: Denial, defensiveness, blaming others, unhealthy physical appearance, bad habits.

Healing: Admitting a problem, prayer (asking for help), immersion in the Word of God, counseling, fellowship, support by loving Christians, acts of God and the Holy Spirit, forgiveness, and love, love and love—through a personal relationship with Christ.

---

1. **Pride and Egotism** *are based on a belief in one's self to the point of saying such things as, Whatever I earn I get; I'm number one; I am a self-made man/woman; I can be anything I want to be; I am woman, I am strong,*

I control my own destiny; I am my own man, and I did it my way. Being proud of your family, business and friends is fine. Being proud without recognizing God and His blessings upon you shows a lack of knowledge. He created each of us. If we use our God-given talents to get ahead or to become successful without sincerely thanking Him for those talents, we are blinded by deceit. We have, in effect, chosen to say, I'm my own god. Typically we are self-centered, concerned about being right (having all the right answers), wanting always to be in control, or looking good, and we get defensive when challenged or when someone defies us, wanting to prove ourselves right.. All these are characteristics of pride gone too far. It is either arrogance or ignorance, apart from God.

2. **Gluttony & Addictions.** *This usually starts with a habit in seeking pleasure because of a spiritual emptiness that only God can fill. As depression or frustration gets worse, the dependency gets stronger. The addiction provides the temporary high for relief; it becomes a "fix" (or god). The addiction is worshipped and develops destructive control over a person's life. Since the addiction is spiritually rooted, it is impossible for anyone to totally overcome this by his own willpower. Changing the addiction to a dependency on God has the greatest chance to produce a successful turnaround. Besides drugs, alcohol, smoking, and food, there are a number of other addictions people might seek (e.g., work, TV, being a sports fanatic, or even simple things like playing or watching golf, tennis or other sports). Aside from drugs, alcohol and smoking, these other activities do not have to be addictive if kept in proper balance, rather than letting them become an addictive release.*

The sorrow of those who run after other gods will increase.

Psalm 16:4

3. **Anger** *can be acquired from a parent or through the seed*

words of bitterness, hate, or jealousy which take root in the spirit, build up and finally are released through yelling or violent acts. Anger is actually a defensive mode in which we fight back out of the fear of being hurt. The deep rooted bitterness or hatred in the heart can only be cured through the healing power of the Word or prayer, which are spiritual. Psychological counseling might help, but it seldom gets to the root of spiritual damage without the Word of God and prayer.

4. **Lust** is an unreasonable desire, most commonly for power, possessions, or sexual release. Sexual desire for a man is a craving and crying out for love. Men, more than women, express love through the sexual act. Sexual lust is a way to fill a spiritual void and hurt. It becomes a passion through mental pictures; that is how pornography, suggestive TV, commercials and clubs perpetuate the problem and stir up cravings.

5. **Laziness** is the lack of motivation found in people with little or no faith in themselves, or the true God. While this can be related to physical energy, it often has more to do with the grip on the heart than with the mind or body. Laziness lets people avoid pain and the fear of failure with other people. Sleeping too much, watching TV excessively, and escaping into food are ways to avoid reality and not having to deal with the fear inside. To God laziness is waste of talent and love.

6. **Envy** is learned from parents and from the deceit of others. It is a hiding place for a damaged heart. People find comfort in "pity parties," wallowing in the hurt they feel of being deprived and short-changed in life. They become paralyzed in their dreams and desires to have what others have, and allow bitterness to develop into resentment for others. Envy is fueled with gossip and breeds more jealousy and hurt.

7. **Greed**—*Money is important and necessary, but it is the love of money which hurts the human spirit. Having money becomes a craving or passion that becomes a measure of self-worth for many individuals. Without money, they consider themselves failures, and they measure the worth of others by it. This attitude creates an imbalance in a person's life because worshipping their idol; money, can destroy a marriage, family, friendship, or a business. God gives some people talent to create capital and wealth, just as he gives an athlete great ability, but if they live their life for this one master it can destroy them in the long run.*

   Many executives who were deprived in their youth have taken on the god of money as a way to overcome the hurt that remains in the underdog *mentality, while others catch the sickness from their parents' attitudes. God wants many of us to be successful financially, but He also wants us to give back generously, not to look at money as a god. Unless you want to be buried in your Cadillac, money will do you no good after your death. Money cannot buy anything eternal.*

These false gods create a situation of trying to *serve two masters.* He created us to serve Himself and others only. Our physical, mental and spiritual makeup is designed for this. We need His help to overcome the influence any false gods which entrap us in a world of deceit.

II. THE 3 CORNERSTONES
OF TRUE WEALTH

The Truth: The first **Cornerstone**, the **Character Truths**, were revealed by God at creation. The second and third **Cornerstones**, **Moral and Spiritual Truths**, were shared as the Ten Commandments by Moses with the Jews, who hungered for direction and a fulfilling new life. As parents, we lay down the law with such commands as *Don't run into the street.* Stop signs and speed limit signs are directions for our conduct. God's Truths are signs for success and danger.

Truths are concerned with what is right and what works to our best benefit, as individuals, families, organizations and nations, over the long run.

**The Spirit
of the Truth:** is the *why*, *how*, and *what to do* of each Truth. Jesus brought and modeled the Spirit of Truth in the New Testament. The "spirit" of every contract has to do with an intent or deeper application beyond the written word. So it is with God's Truths; He looks at our motives, actions and willingness to be obedient in relationship to these truths, as we let the Holy Spirit work in us.

**Character
Quality:** As God's command to *take on His image* illustrates, He wants us to exemplify His character. Each truth has an application to bring us closer to living according to His purposes, character and righteousness.

Forgiveness: is required by God. Matthew 6:14-15 says, *If you won't forgive others, you offend God's creation, thus offending Him. He will not forgive you.* Matthew 7:12 says, *So in everything, do to others what you would have them to do to you, for this sums up the law and the prophets.* (This is the Golden Rule) *This is love for God: to obey his commands, and His commands are not burdensome, for everyone born of God overcomes the world, you can't love God and hate your brother.*
John 5:3

THE TRUTH *Genesis 1:26* *(paraphrased)*	THE SPIRIT OF THE TRUTH	CHARACTER QUALITY
I. God created man in His image.	I created you in love and grace: • To be righteous. • To love and be loved. • To be kind and patient. • To be accountable and forgiving. • To be a light to others. • To love and enjoy life. • To think long term. • To model My character, as Jesus did. • To learn from your trials.	Take on His character of love, truth and light.
II. Be fruitful and increase.	• To multiply, reproduce, profit. • To plant, nurture, harvest. • To create, discover and enjoy. • To grow personally and share with others. • To learn and respect the use of My resources.	Create and invest for growth.
III. Fill and subdue the earth.	• To plan, delegate, build, control. • To take initiative, be aggressive and do your best • To use your personality, intelligence, skills, natural desires. • To witness, carry My name to the ends of the earth.	Put your talents to work.
IV. Rule over every living creature.	• To make laws, lead, be responsible for truth. • To communicate, teach, and be an example. • To establish principles and rules to live by. • To be tough when necessary in love and sacrifice.	Lead by example.

Character Truths

We are given dominion and asked to take initiative, yet we are created to need God. He keeps spiritual controls of heaven and earth.

THE TRUTH	THE SPIRIT OF THE TRUTH	CHARACTER QUALITY
	Jesus said, *"Secondly, love your neighbor as yourself."* (Referred to also as "The Golden Rule")	
I. Honor your father and mother.	• Love, honor and forgive your mother, father, spouse and children because they represent My plan for families and organizations. • Every organization is a family where authority should be respected, honored and followed. • Pray for those in authority.	Respect authority as family.
II. You shall not murder.	• Build relationships with others. • Love your fellowman, no matter how he offends you. • Life and death is My decision, not yours. • Forgiveness will heal your heart.	Forgive and value life.
III. You shall not commit adultery.	• Love and be fruitful to those you have joined in covenant. • Abstain from impure relationships until commitment, true love, for My purposes. • Honor your employer and employees with love, respect and fairness.	Be faithful and loyal.
IV. You shall not steal.	• Give to others and it will be given unto you. • I will bless you bountifully for loving and protecting your fellowman. • Tithe to prove your love to Me. • Your motive will be judged.	Give to others.
V. Do not bear false witness.	• Respect your fellowman by being honest with him in all things. • Communicate with integrity, do not withhold truth. • Be open to listen with discernment for I will use your fellowman to confirm My intentions.	Earn respect through integrity.
VI. You shall not covet the goods of others.	• Pray that your fellowman and his family will be richly blessed, prosper and grow without regard to your desires. • I will provide for your needs according to My plan. • Every man's talents, skills, abilities, personality, and physical features will be different and have unique rewards.	Appreciate and encourage others.

Moral Truth Toward Man
Moral truths about the relationship between you and your fellowman will affect the continued success of any individual, family, organization or nation.

Spiritual Truths Toward God
Spiritual truths are about a personal relationship with the Lord, and about doing His will.

THE TRUTH The Ten Commandments Deuteronomy 5:6-21 (paraphrased)	THE SPIRIT OF THE TRUTH The New Testament (paraphrased) *Jesus said, "Love your God with all your heart and all your might."*	CHARACTER QUALITY
I. Have no other Gods.	• Love me as your God, put Me first in your life and I will fill your spirit and give you visions. • Be open and humble to My leading. • Pride before Me will cause emptiness, stress and unfruitfulness. • Only I, as your Creator, know your needs. • Worry not, but put your trust in Me.	Be humble and trust Him.
II. Have no false idols.	• As God, I am spirit, love, truth and light. • I am not represented by superstitions, statues, people, material wealth or physical objects. • I am a jealous God, so heed My words. • Generations will be affected by your love for Me. • No one can serve two masters; watch what you worship.	Be convicted and forgiven.
III. Don't use God's name in vain.	• Honor Me with thanksgiving, praise, and prayer. • My name is Holy and commands power. • Preserve My name in the hearts of your people. • Your words create and command good and evil. • Life and death is in the power of the tongue.	Praise with your words.
IV. Keep the Sabbath holy.	• Plan to rest and spend time with Me. • My word, prayer and fellowship will teach you. • Love, peace, joy and wisdom will come to those who grow close to Me.	Rest and listen in Him.

255

III. Three Cornerstone Expectations by Biblical Standards
...the Patterns of Success

Character Truth *Character of Love*	Moral Truth *Love One Another*	Spiritual Truth *Loving God*
His Image Fill and Subdue Fruitful and Increase Rule Over	Honor Mother and Father Not Murder Not Steal No Adultery No False Witness Not Covet	No Other God No False Idols Not Use Name In Vain Observe the Sabbath
Our Duties and Responsibilihes Achieving Our Potential	Our Relationship with Others	Our Relationships with Him

Personal Relationship
Following Him
Taking Direction
Vision & Wisdom
Security
Discernment & Insight
Higher Purpose
Listening & Hearing
Prayer & Praise
Learning & Growing
Peace & Fulfillment
Joy & Contentment
Holy Spirit Reliance

ROI – Results
Blessing, Void or Pain

'DESCRIPTORS'

Interpersonal Relationships
Communication & Feedback
Support & Sharing
Confirmation & Correction
Delegation & Leverage
Teamwork & Family
Giving Direction
Honesty & Promise
Integrity & Follow Through
Forgiveness
Self Discipline

ROI – Results
Blessing, Void or Pain

'DESCRIPTORS'

Character & Integrity
Attitude & Experience
Talents & Gifts
Intelligence & Ability
Achievement & Performance
Work Ethic
Leadership
Responsibility
Initiative & Risk
Acquired Knowledge
Confidence &
Personal Growth

ROI – Results
Blessing, Void or Pain

IV. The Johari Window

ME (self)

Things I Know   *Things I Don't Know*

YOU (individual or group)

Things You Know

Things You Don't Know

Open Arena	Blind Spot
Facade (Hidden Arena)	Unknown

The **Johari Window** is often used in management circles to illustrate the needs for teamwork, good communications, relationships where people help one another and focus in the right area or priorities for betterment or productivity.

This simple illustration also applies to the Three Corner-stones of Truth. Let us show you how.

(Johari Window was developed by psychologists Joe Luft and Harry Ingham in 1955, Western Training Labs, University of California.)

Open arena–things I know and publicly share, so others will know them as well, while other things are obvious, i.e., appearance, manners, talents, abilities, etc.

Character–Our character shows. As we come to know people we see how they walk their talk and live up to their potential.

Facade (hidden arena)–Things we know about ourselves but are not willing to share with others, i.e., faults, background, inner desires/motives. Here we play roles, our fear is looking stupid so we put on a front to others.

Blind Spot–Here's an area where we can't see some things which are more obvious to others, "our back side," i.e., personal weaknesses, misunderstandings, mistakes we are about to make, lack of knowledge or experience, naiveness.

Moral–Loving your neighbor is communication with a desire to help, grow, serve and improve together.

Unknown–Areas that neither of us know or can predict or project, i.e., your business is about to lose an important customer, you are about to become very sick, a new opportunity or friend is just around the corner.

Spiritual–Only God knows, but trust in Him gives us peace, insights, discernment and vision in the ups and downs of life or business.

V. ILLUSTRATIONS OF FOUNDATIONS

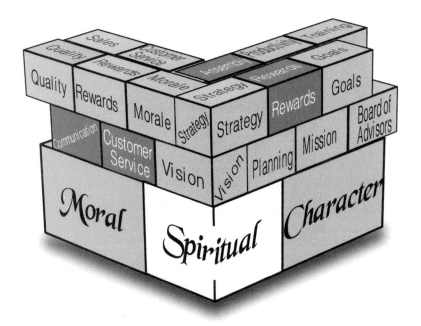

The Solid Foundation

The business built on a solid foundation of the Three Cornerstones of Truth will prosper in good times and bad. Making big profits are not always a sign of true wealth.

Truths also apply to:

- Individuals
- Families
- Nations

They must also build their existence on the right Cornerstones of Truth. Reference also, Character Traits.

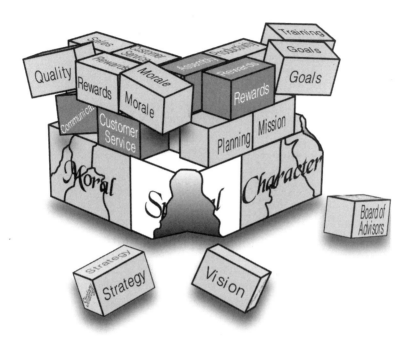

The Cracking Foundation

The business built on a cracking or broken foundation of people not following Truth will eventually suffer and crumble. Only the blessings, prayers of some people may keep it together until it can revive.

80% of small businesses fail. Big businesses decline, reorganize, heal, sell or merge, or die without living by Truth.

VI. *THE BEGINNING STEPS TO TRUE WEALTH BY THE BOOK*

God knows your heart and is not as concerned with your words as He is with the attitude of your heart. The following is a suggested prayer to get closer to God:

> *Lord Jesus, I need You. Thank You for dying on the cross for my sins. I open the door of my life and receive You as my Savior and Lord. Thank You for forgiving my sins and giving me eternal life. Take control of the throne of my life. Make me the kind of person You want me to be.*

SUGGESTIONS FOR CHRISTIAN GROWTH

Spiritual growth results from trusting Jesus Christ. *The righteous man shall live by faith.* (Galatians 3:11) A life of faith will enable you to trust God increasingly with every detail of your life, and to practice the following:

G *Go to God in prayer daily* (John 15:7).

R *Read God's Word daily* (Acts 17:11)—begin with the Gospel of John.

O *Obey God moment by moment* (John 14:21).

W *Witness for Christ by your life and words* (Matthew 4:19; John 15:8).

T *Trust God for every detail of your life* (1 Peter 5:7).

H *The Holy Spirit - allow Him to control and empower your daily life and witness* (Galatians 5:16,17; Acts 1:8).

FELLOWSHIP IN A GOOD CHURCH

God's Word admonishes us not to forsake "the assembling of ourselves together" (Hebrews 10:25). Several logs burn brightly together; but put one aside on the cold hearth and the fire goes out. So it is with your relationship with other Christians. If you do not belong to a church, do not wait to be invited. Take the initiative; call the pastor of a nearby church where Christ is honored and His Bible is taught. Start this week, and make plans to attend regularly.

Reprinted from *The Four Spiritual Laws*, *Campus Crusade for Christ.*

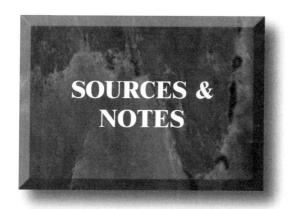

Overall Sources

The Holy Spirit, Bible and Prayer. Personal Interviews, tapes, articles, speeches, broadcasts and books.

Introduction

The Holy Bible, American Bible Society, NY, NY.

Chapter 1

- *Henry P. Crowell* by Richard Ellsworth Day, *Breakfast Table Autocrat*, Moody Press, 1946.
- Dave Dravecky, *Hope in the Midst of Adversity*, Life Story, Sumas, Washington, 1994.
- J. C. Penney, *Man with a Thousand Partners*, Harper, NY, NY, 1931.
- George Rogers, *The Art of Virtue*, Acorn Publishing, Eden Prairie, MN, 1990. (Ben Franklin story).
- Truett Cathy, *Serving the Lord in Business*, Focus on the Family, Colorado Springs, CO, 1992.
- Martin Luther King, Jr. *Martin Luther King, Jr. Companion*, St. Martin's Press, NY, NY 1995.
- Rick DeVos, *Compassionate Capitalism*, Penguin Group, NY, NY 1993.
- John Wooden, *My First Seven Points*, Fellowship of Christian Athletes, Kansas City, MO, 1990.
- Joe Gibbs, *The Proof's in the Power*, Fellowship of Christian Athletes, Kansas City, MO, 1990.
- Character Training Institute, Oklahoma City, OK.

Chapter 2
- Horatio Alger Association of Distinguished Americans, Alexandria, VA, April, 1997.

Chapter 3
- Randy Pennington & Marc Bockman, *On My Honor, I Will*, Treasure House, Shippenstary, PA, 1995. (Sam Walton story).
- Orville Redenbacher, *The Funny Looking Farmer with the Funny Sounding Name, Guideposts*, NY, NY, January 1990.
- Bob Nourse, *Origins of The Executive Committee (TEC)*, Milwaukee, WI, 1990.
- Mary Kay, *Mary Kay— You Can Have it All*, Prima Publishers, Rocklin, CA, 1995.
- Jewel Abels, *Rockefeller Billions*, MacMillan, NY, NY, 1965. (John D. Rockefeller story).
- Bill Pollard, *The Soul of the Firm*, Co-Published by Harper Business and Zondervan, Division of Harper Collins Publishers, 1996.
- Joe Gibbs, *A Game Plan for Life*, Life Story, Sumas, Washington, 1995.

Chapter 4
- Frederick Phillips, *Business Ethics for True Profitability*, Executive Leadership Foundation, Atlanta, GA, 1992.
- Ronald Reagan, *Speaking My Mind*, Simon & Schuster, NY, NY, 1989.
- George Washington, *America's Godly Heritage*, Wallbuilders Press, Aledo, TX, 1992.
- Ted Koppel, *The Last Word at Duke University*, ABC News, NY, NY, 1987.
- Conrad Hilton, *America on its Knees, Be My Guest*, Prentice Hall, 1957, reprinted by Fireside Books, NY, NY, 1994.

Chapter 5
- J. C. Penney, *50 Years of the Golden Rule*, Harper & Row, NY, NY, 1950.
- Cecil B. deMille, *How Faith Learned as a Boy Guided My Career, Guideposts*, NY, NY, 1954.
- Mary Kay, *Mary Kay—You Can Have it All*, ibid.
- Randy Pennington & Marc Bockman, *On My Honor, I Will*, ibid. (Jessie Shwayder story).
- Julius Erving, Fellowship of Christian Athletes, Kansas City, MO 1986.

- Richard Kughn, *Like a Kid in a Candy Store, Guideposts*, NY, NY, December 1990.

Chapter 6

- Adolph Coors, IV, *No Right to Hate*, Voice Speaks About, Gift Publications, Costa Mesa, CA, 1989.
- Jim Moran, *Florida Chamber News*, Florida Chamber of Commerce, Tallahassee, FL, March, 1996.
- Peter Hay, *The Book of Business Anecdotes*, Wing Books, Avenel, NJ, 1988. (Tom Watson story).
- Robert Townsend, *Further up the Organization.*
- Homer Figler, *My Minister Meant Business, Guideposts*, NY, NY, April, 1984.
- Sam Walton, *Sam Walton —Made in America*, Bantam Audio Publishing, NY, NY, 1992.

Chapter 7

- Lee Ezell, *Answers to Life's Missing Pieces*, Life Story, Sumas, Washington, 1995.
- Frederick E. Reichheld, *The Loyalty Effect*, Harvard Business School, Boston, MA, 1996.
- Charlie & Dotty Duke, *Walk on the Moon, Walk with the Son*, Sumas, Washington, 1993.
- Michelle Quinn, *Today's CEO: Focused, Domineering, Tireless, San Jose Mercury News*, San Jose, CA, June 24, 1996.
- Randy Pennington & Marc Bockman, *On My Honor I Will*, ibid. (Manville quote).
- Jack Eckerd, *Finding the Right Prescription*, JME, Clearwater, FL 1987.

Chapter 8

- S.I. McMillen, *None of these Diseases*, ibid. (John D. Rockefeller story).
- Mortimer Feinberg, Ph.D. and John J. Tarrant, *Why Smart People Do Dumb Things*, Fireside, NY, NY, 1995. (Stew Leonard story).
- *Christian Herald* Magazine, January 1992. (Jack Eckerd story).
- *International Pirating, Wall Street Journal*, Dow Jones Corp, NY, NY, April 20, 1996.
- Wally Amos, *The Calling Card, Guideposts*, NY, NY, March 1985.
- Bill Pollard, *The Soul of the Firm*, ibid.

Chapter 9

- David Schwartz, *Truth - It's Good Business, Guideposts*, NY, NY, January 1985.
- Paul DeVries and Barry Gardner, *The Taming of the Shrewd*, Thomas Nelson, Nashville, TN, 1992. (Beechnut story).
- Frank Abagnale, *Catch Me if You Can*, Focus on the Family, Colorado Springs, CO, 1993.
- Peter Hay, *The Book of Business Anecdotes*, ibid. (Abraham Lincoln story).
- Ken Wessner, *The Soul of the Firm*, ibid.

Chapter 10

- Jackie Robinson, *Trouble Ahead Needn't Bother You, Guideposts* Book, NY, NY, 1954.
- Pricie Hanna, *The New Vice President, Guideposts*, NY, NY, August 1986.
- Bill Cosby, *Are You Dead?*, C-SPAN, Viewer Services, Washington, DC, April 8, 1996.
- Dr. Laura Nash, *Believers in Business*, , ibid. (Andy Story).

Chapter 11

- Dr. Laura Nash, *Believers in Business*, Thomas Nelson Publishers, Nashville, TN, 1994.
- Richard Hagberg *Rambos in Pinstripes: Why so Many CEOs are Lousy Leaders, Fortune* Magazine, Chicago, IL, June 24, 1996.
- Bob Bowerman, *The Kitchen - Table Shoemaker, Guideposts*, NY, NY, January, 1988.
- James L. Kraft, *Pattern for Prosperity, Guideposts*, NY, NY, 1954.

Chapter 12

- Mary Kay, *Mary Kay—You Can Have it All*, ibid.
- Louis E. Boone, *Abraham Lincoln, Success & Failure, Quotable Business*, Random House, New York, NY, 1992.
- Jack Stack, *Great Game of Business*, TEC, Florida, 1994.
- John F. Love, *McDonald's Behind the Arches*, Bantam Books, NY, NY, 1995.
- Bobby Bowden, "Coach as Christian", *Living Words*, Jacksonville, FL 1991.
- Pete Maravich, "There is Life after the NBA," Fellowship of Christian Athletes, Kansas City, MO.

- Charles Colson, *Thank God for Watergate*, Life Story, Sumas, Washington, 1993.
- Ronald Reagan, *Speaking My Mind*, ibid.
- Oprah Winfrey, Wellesley College Commencement, C-SPAN, Washington, D.C., May 30, 1997.

Chapter 13

- Robert Schuller, *Believe in the God Who Believes in You*, Thomas Nelson, Nashville, TN, 1989.
- Dr. Ken Cooper, *It's Better to Believe*, Thomas Nelson, Nashville, TN 1995.
- S.I. McMillen, *Love or Perish, None of these Diseases*, M.D. Revell, Grand Rapids, MI, Revised 1995.
- Scott to Carson, Horatio Alger Association of Distinguished Americans, Alexandria, VA, April, 1997.

Chapter 14

- Conrad Hilton, *Be My Guest*, Prentice Hall, 1957; republished by Fireside Books, NY, NY, 1994.
- Grant Teaff, *Finding God's Will in a Plane Crash*, Fellowship of Christian Athletes, Kansas City, MO.
- Robert Schuller, *Believe in the God Who Believes in You*, ibid.
- Pete Maravich, *There is Life After the NBA*, ibid.
- Dr. Ken Cooper, *It's Better to Believe*, ibid.
- Tom Landry, Fellowship of Christian Athletes, Kansas City, MO 1986.
- Bobby Bowden, *Coach as a Christian*, ibid.
- Ken Blanchard, *We are the Beloved*, Zondervan Publishing, Grand Rapids, MI, 1994.

Chapter 15

- David F. Miller , J. C. Penney story, used with permission, 1987.
- Paul Anka, C. Francois, J. Revaux & G. Thibault, *My Way*.

Illustrations

- Many quotes from *God's Little Illustration Book*, Honor Book, Tulsa, OK 1993.
- Some quotes from *God's Chicken Soup for the Spirit*.
- William D. Lawrence with Jack A. Turpin, *Beyond the Bottom Line*, Praxis Books, Moody Press, Chicago, IL, 1994.

ABOUT THE AUTHOR
AND THE BELIEVERS, INC.

John F. Beehner is an entrepreneur, having started four different businesses. His 12 years as founder and CEO of TEC Florida (The Executive Committee) afforded him a rare opportunity to individually work with over one hundred different CEOs of small to mid-size companies.

The purpose of TEC is to ultimately help executives improve their leadership skills, company performance and profitability. Under John's leadership, TEC assembled a staff of twenty, working with more than 300 executives monthly. The parent company is the largest business of its kind, with offices and staff in fifty cities in the United States and ten foreign countries.

John's spiritual journey began in 1982 and led him to the TEC business. In 1995, he received a vision to combine his practical business experience with the insight he received through prayer and scripture. John believes his experience with strategy, motivation, marketing and management combined with the insight of purpose, peace, love and success, will help executives understand God's design for a rapidly changing world hungry for the Truth.

He sold his majority interest in TEC to pursue the publication of the first edition of this book. John spent one and a half years researching this book, now in its third edition.

The Believers, Inc.

The Believers, Inc. is an organization designed to help business executives implement Biblical Truths in their lives and marketplace. Companies, churches, and associations are invited to inquire about our workshop or seminar programs. Opportunities for executives and consultants wanting to teach, lead, and facilitate sessions are available through our training, licensing, and support programs.

Audio and video tapes will be available as well. Phone toll free:

1 (888) 847-3861.

TRUE WEALTH
...By The Book

The 3 Cornerstones of Truth

1. Character Truths:

God created man in His image
>Take on His character of love, truth, and light

Be fruitful and increase
>Create and invest for growth

Fill and subdue the earth
>Put your talents to work

Rule over every living creature
>Lead by example

2. Moral Truths:

>Jesus said, "Love your neighbor"

Honor your father and mother
>Respect authority as family

Do not murder
>Forgive and value life

Do not commit adultery
>Be faithful and loyal

Do not steal
>Give to others

Do not bear false witness
>Earn respect through integrity

Do not covet
>Appreciate and encourage others

3. Spiritual Truths:

>Jesus said, "Love God"

Have no other gods
>Be humble and trust Him

Have no false idols
>Be convicted and forgiven

Don't use His name in vain
>Praise with your words

Keep the Sabbath holy
>Rest and listen in Him